The Nature of the Church

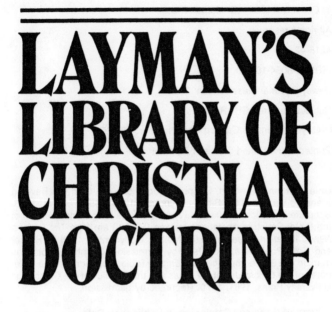

LAYMAN'S LIBRARY OF CHRISTIAN DOCTRINE

The Nature of the Church
BILL J. LEONARD

BROADMAN PRESS
Nashville, Tennessee

Library of Congress Cataloging-in-Publication Data

Leonard, Bill.
  The nature of the church.

  (Layman's library of Christian doctrine ; 12)
  Includes index.
    1. Church.   2. Baptists—Doctrines.   I. Title.
II. Series.
BV600.2.L46   1986   262'.7   86-17574
ISBN 0-8054-1642-0

Foreword

The *Layman's Library of Christian Doctrine* in sixteen volumes covers the major doctrines of the Christian faith.

To meet the needs of the lay reader, the *Library* is written in a popular style. Headings are used in each volume to help the reader understand which part of the doctrine is being dealt with. Technical terms, if necessary to the discussion, will be clearly defined.

The need for this series is evident. Christians need to have a theology of their own, not one handed to them by someone else. The *Library* is written to help readers evaluate and form their own beliefs based on the Bible and on clear and persuasive statements of historic Christian positions. The aim of the series is to help laymen hammer out their own personal theology.

The books range in size from 140 pages to 168 pages. Each volume deals with a major part of Christian doctrine. Although some overlap is unavoidable, each volume will stand on its own. A set of the sixteen-volume series will give a person a complete look at the major doctrines of the Christian church.

Each volume is personalized by its author. The author will show the vitality of Christian doctrines and their meaning for everyday life. Strong and fresh illustrations will hold the interest of the reader. At times the personal faith of the authors will be seen in illustrations from their own Christian pilgrimage.

Not all laymen are aware they are theologians. Many may believe they know nothing of theology. However, every person believes something. This series helps the layman to understand what he believes and to be able to be "prepared to make a defense to anyone who calls him to account for the hope that is in him" (1 Pet. 3:15, RSV).

Contents

Contents

1

What Is the Church?

Upon this rock I will build my church; and the gates of hell shall not prevail against it (Matt. 16:18, KJV).

For where the church is, there is the Spirit of God; and where the Spirit of God is, there is the church, and every kind of grace.

—Iranaeus, second-century bishop

By the fact that they [Christians] themselves admit that these people are worthy of their God, they show that they are want and able to "convince only the foolish, dishonourable and stupid, and only slaves, women, and little children."

—Celsus, second-century pagan philosopher

Now this Church is the congregation of the saints, in which the Gospel is rightly taught and the sacraments rightly administered.

—Martin Luther, sixteenth-century preacher

Too much of the work of the Church today is like a squirrel in a cage—lots of activity, but no progress.

Billy Sunday, twentieth-century evangelist

The Church: Ideal and Real

Perhaps the church has always had an "image" problem. Its lofty gospel of salvation, love, and servanthood truly seems good news until human beings enter the picture. Even with the best intentions, the people of God turn all too quickly from the dynamic ideal of the gospel to the worldliness, hypocrisy, or boredom of the human condition.

The apostle Paul set forth that ideal when he wrote that Christ "loved the church" and "gave himself up for her, that he might sanctify her, having cleansed her by the washing of water with the word, that he might present the church to himself in splendor, without spot or wrinkle, or any such thing, that she might be holy and without blemish" (Eph. 5:25-27).

Paul also recognized the reality of the church's humanity when he wrote to the "foolish Galatians" (Gal 3:1): "I am astonished that you are so quickly deserting him who called you in the grace of Christ and turning to a different gospel" (1:6). From its very beginning, the church has had difficulty living in light of the gospel.

Like its Lord, the church is both human and divine. It is divine in that it is the body of Christ, the continuing sign of God's work in the world. It is human in that it bears the marks of humanity—fallibility, mortality, brokenness, and vulnerability.[1] Unlike its Lord, the church experiences sin and must continually turn to Christ for forgiveness and reconciliation. Yet with that restoration, the church carries out Christ's work in the world. As Harold DeWolf wrote: "As Jesus was a man, so the church is of earth and like him, a bridge between earth and heaven, with the power and love of God flowing down through it out into the world."[2]

The church of Jesus Christ, therefore, is no mere abstract ideal. Its work of reconciliation is expressed in the real world with real sinners called to grace. Its gospel can be taken seriously because it is given to sinful, imperfect human beings. Thus we cannot love the idea of the church unless we are willing to love the people who are the church. As Richard J. Neuhaus wrote, "To love abstractions is not to love at all; it is but a sentimental attachment to our own whimsies."[3]

The relationship between the ideal and the real means that there is always tension between the "faith of the church and our experience of the church."[4] The faith of the church is a confidence in God who is the author of salvation and the source of the church's life. Our experience of the church is conditioned by the limitations and mortality of its earthly members. Through faith in God, we can experience those spiritual gifts which the church offers while recognizing that they are sometimes limited, even fragmented, by the church's immediate frailties and imperfections.

The Church: A Diversity of Traditions

Whether in abstract ideal or day-to-day reality, defining or even describing the nature of the church is no easy matter. For one thing, there are all of those churches within the church, characterized by a diversity of doctrine and tradition that seems almost irreconcilable. Worship practices extend from the elaborate ritual and liturgy of Eastern Orthodox, Roman Catholic, or Anglican traditions, to the organized spontaneity of Pentecostal/charismatic churches, to the silent simplicity of the Quakers.

Episcopalians, Lutherans, Catholics, and others administer baptism to infants and adults; Southern Baptists and Pentecostals baptize children and adults, while Mennonites baptize adult believers only. Quakers and members of the Salvation Army do not baptize at all. In some churches, the bread and cup of the Lord's Supper serve as a memorial to Christ; others receive those "elements" as the very body and blood of the Lord, while still others "feed on Christ" spiritually as a witness of the "inner light." Two-Seed-in-the-Spirit Predestinarian Baptists declare that salvation is given only to the elect whom God has chosen before the foundation of the world. Free Will Baptists believe that "whosoever will" may choose to receive God's grace. Having once chosen Christ, believers may later reject Him, turn from salvation, and "fall from grace." Some churches have elaborate hierarchies, others mirror corporate business organizations, while others shun all organizational structure for fear of conformity to the world. And so it goes.

Where, then, is the "true" church amid the diversity of all the churches? The church is one because Christ is one. Those who are bound to Christ are bound to His church and to each other. The church is diverse because no one community of faith or communion of belief, no one congregation or denomination, can fulfill all the gospel, all at once. Diverse forms of the church exist, not because the gospel is relative or "watered down" to fit every possible circumstance, but because it is relevant, responsive to the diverse needs of persons, cultures, and societies.

What Is the Church?: A Variety of Answers

Not only are there all those churches, there are also innumerable attitudes and opinions about what the church is and ought to be. Indeed, the question, "What is the church?" produces a variety of answers from persons inside and outside the community of faith. The following are but a few of the most representative views.

Church as Inevitable Failure

For some, the church is an inevitable failure. It presents an ideal which it is unable to realize or implement. Its gospel has become so institution-alized, so captivated by culture, as to be irreconcilable with the simple faith taught by Jesus of Nazareth. Critics thus point to the church's sanction of war, inquisition, and ignorance, its overwhelming concern for the status quo, and its continued compromise with the world as evidence of its failure. For them, the church has failed to live up to the prophetic vision and self-sacrificing service of its Founder. It is so far from the gospel ideal as to be irreconcilable with the simple teachings of Jesus.

Church as a Matter of Indifference

Others—perhaps a growing number of persons in Western Society—are not antagonistic toward the church. They are simply indifferent to it. The church is not a great moral failure; it is just another way of coping with life. It may be an acceptable institution for those who want to prac-tice religion, attend services, or discuss religious issues but it is not a necessary element for meaningful life. Those who view the church this way have no quarrel with religion; they are simply not "into" church activities. The church and its gospel make no impact on their lives. They do not pay much attention to it at all. Indifference may pose the most serious challenge for the church in contemporary society.

Church as a Source of Stability

Some view the church as a source of social order and stability which, along with home, family, schools, and other community institutions, helps perpetuate values, morality, and virtue within human civilization. The church guides persons in understanding their relation-ship to the community and accepting responsibility for their behavior in society. It is an enduring institution which bridges the generations by providing a source of continuity with the past and identity in the present. The particular doctrines and practices of the various churches are less significant than the common values promoted by the Christian commu-nity within society as a whole. While this view has merit, those who support it may not necessarily recognize the spiritual dimension of the church as people of God. Church is merely one of many institutions which provide stability and order in human society.

Church as Religious Ghetto

For some persons, the church is a religious ghetto, a "place" where one goes to be religious, talk religious, and act religious. Christian commitment may be evaluated primarily in terms of support for and attendance of a wide variety of programs and activities within the religious setting. Some may even refer to the church in terms of location—"our church plant" or "our facilities." Church is a place of protection from the onslaughts of the sinful world and a community of participation in which Christianity and church attendance become almost synonymous.

Truly church is closely related to place. Locale becomes a tangible expression of continuing community and spiritual resources. Yet the church is not bound by location or program. Christianity involves participation in the community of faith but also active response to the needs of the world. The church is not an escape; it is a place which nourishes us for life and ministry in the world.

Church as Corporate Institution

Still others act as if the identifying mark of the church is its corporate institutionalism. The church is therefore a well-structured organization, dispensing a service (Christian ministry) and promoting a product (Christianity). Ministers are ecclesiastical chief executives whose effectiveness is evaluated in terms of growth in the program, budget, and participation in the life of the religious corporation.

The church needs organization, true enough. Some institutionalization is almost inevitable for implementing the church's mission. At its heart, however, the church is not a corporation but a community of faith. If institutionalism creates a loss of spiritual renewal and "flexibility," the church may well gain the world but lose its own soul, its unique identity in Christ.[5]

Church as Spiritual Communion

One other view of the church perhaps incorporates the best of earlier views within a broader context of faith and practice. The church in its best and most basic sense is a spiritual communion, concerned with the whole life of humanity—spiritual, institutional, social, moral, and communal. It is local yet universal; individual yet corporate; an ideal to be sought and a reality to be practiced. It is a "place," not necessarily a structure or a building, but always a tangible community in which persons are accepted, forgiven, redeemed, nurtured, and instructed in the life of the gospel, the good news of Jesus Christ. As James Gustafson observed, the "continuation of the common inner life and spirit requires the guidance, informing power, and judgment of the particular organized congregation."[6] In this way spirit and form work together. Obviously, these views are not the only approaches to the nature of the church, nor is each necessarily exclusive of the other. They often exist in various forms among varied persons.

The church interprets the gospel for the individual within community. Yet the church is not simply a community of believers but a community of believers in Jesus. It is not simply a community which serves others but a community which serves others in the name of Jesus. All which the church is and does is informed by God's activity in Jesus Christ.

What Is the Church?: A People on a Journey

What is the church? In brief, it is a historical community which begins with God and is founded on Jesus Christ. It is witness to His gospel in its worship, and faith, work and memory. Through its witness in word and servanthood it points beyond itself to Christ. "It is a community which is being redeemed and at the same time a means of redemption."[7]

This book examines the nature of the church in its biblical, historical, and theological contexts. The recurring theme of this study is that the nature of the church is a paradox. It is bound by elements which must continually be held in creative tension. The forces of freedom and authority, law and gospel, spontaneity and order, must ever be kept in balance within the community of faith. Yet maintaining such balance is a constant challenge for the church. Law can deteriorate to legalism; authority may turn to authoritarianism; freedom turns to license; and concern for order succumbs to compromise with the world. Evangelism becomes simply a means for recruitment while the primary efforts of the church are increasingly directed toward preserving its own structures of power rather than losing itself for the sake of the gospel. As H. Richard Niebuhr observed, the church "loses its character—as the church—when it concentrates on itself, worships itself and seeks to make love of the church the first commandment."[8]

The church, therefore, lives by paradox, that effort to hold in balance the powerful and creative forces of the spiritual life. In so doing the church is continually in process. It is a bride being prepared for Christ (2 Cor. 11:2); it is a community of pilgrims, chosen, but not yet complete, ever moving toward the promise of the kingdom of God. "We are the Church," one scholar wrote, "and if we are the Church, then the Church is a fellowship of those who seek, journey and lose their way, of the helpless, the anguished and the suffering, of sinners and pilgrims."[9]

The pilgrimage we share is not ours alone. It belongs to a community which extends throughout time, which is ever related to Christ and His people, past, present, and future. The faith which we profess is not ours alone but belongs to all those in every time and place who take up the cross and follow Christ. The consequences of that pilgrimage and the faith on which it is begun is what this book is about. To ask the question "What is the church?" is no mere academic exercise or abstract theological speculation. It is to ask questions about God, about life, and about ourselves. It is to seek "for a city which hath foundations, whose builder and maker is God" (Heb. 11:10, KJV).

Notes

1. Collin Williams, *The Church* (Philadelphia: The Westminster Press, 1968), p. 73.

2. Harold DeWolf, *A Hard Rain and a Cross* (Nashville: Abingdon Press, 1966), p. 104.

3. Richard John Neuhaus, *Freedom For Ministry*, p. 12.

4. Jürgen Moltmann, *The Church in the Power of the Holy Spirit*, p. 20.

5. Stephen Rose, *The Grass Roots Church* (Nashville: Abingdon Press, 1966), p. 17.

6. James Gustafson, *Treasure in Earthen Vessels: The Church as a Human Community* (New York: Harper, 1961), p. 102.

7. John Dillenberger and Claude Welch, *Protestant Christianity* (New York: Charles Scribner's Sons, 1954), p. 322.

8. H. Richard Niebuhr, *The Purpose of the Church and Its Ministry* (New York: Harper and Brothers, 1956), p. 30.

9. Hans Küng, *The Church*, p. 33.

Suggested Readings

Flew, R. Newton. *Jesus and His Church*. New York: Abingdon Press, 1938.

Hinson, E. Glenn. *The Integrity of the Church*. Nashville: Broadman Press, 1978.

Küng, Hans. *The Church*. New York: Sheed and Ward, 1967.

McCall, Duke, ed. *What Is the Church?* Nashville: Broadman Press, 1968.

Miller, Donald G. *The Nature and Mission of the Church*. Richmond: John Knox Press, 1957.

Minear, Paul. *Images of the Church in the New Testament*. Philadelphia: Westminster Press, 1960.

Moltmann, Jürgen. *The Church in the Power of the Holy Spirit*. New York: Harper and Row, Publishers, 1977.

Nelson, J. Robert. *The Realm of Redemption*. Greenwich, Connecticut: The Seabury Press, 1951.

Neuhaus, Richard John. *Freedom for Ministry*. New York: Harper and Row, 1979.

Paul, Robert S. *The Church in Search of Itself*. Grand Rapids, Mich.: William B. Eerdmans Publishing Company, 1972.

Willimon, William. *What's Right with the Church?* New York: Harper and Row, Publishers, 1985.

2

Jesus Christ, Head of the Church

Jesus Christ is head of the church. All ecclesiology rests on that basic truth. Without Christ there is no church. There is no other foundation on which the church may build (1 Cor. 3:11). Thus the doctrine of the church (ecclesiology) is inseparable from the doctrine of Christ (Christology). As Jürgen Moltmann wrote, "There is only a church if and as long as Jesus of Nazareth is believed and acknowledged to be the Christ of God."[1] The authority of the church is derived only from Christ. The work of the church is Christ's work; the gospel of the church is Christ's gospel. He is the measure by which the church judges itself and is judged by God. The church is Christian only so far as Christ Himself is the source and goal of the church's teaching and ministry. Everything which the church does is informed by God's activity in Christ.

Christian history details the continued struggle of God's people to conform to the image of Christ and retain unity with Him amid the distractions of the world. In each new era, the church must return to the basic question of who Jesus is and what His life, death, and resurrection mean to His people. Therefore, the doctrine of the church is based essentially on "God's revelation of himself."[2] The study of the church begins and ends with Jesus Christ.

A Community Before Jesus

A Historic Faith

To say that the church is founded on Jesus Christ means that Christianity is a historic faith. The early Christians believed that they were a community rooted, not in abstract speculation, but in a historic event, the

17

incarnation. Jesus was no mere figment of the church's imagination but a divine presence who took on flesh and entered human history. Paul wrote that, "when the fulness of the time was come, God sent forth his Son, made of a woman, made under the law" (Gal. 4:4, KJV). Christians believe that human history is the arena of God's activity. Through the incarnation of Jesus Christ, the Lord of history entered history itself.

A community with a past.—As a community grounded in history, the first-century Christians believed that they were the fulfillment of that historic faith first revealed to Israel. The church which gathered around Jesus of Nazareth was heir to the promise which God had made to the Israelites. "In many and various ways God spoke of old to our fathers by the prophets; but in these last days he has spoken to us by a Son" (Heb. 1:1).

The church, while a truly new creation, was not without a past. A community of faithful people existed long before Jesus appeared in history. E. Clinton Gardner suggested, "From its beginnings the church has understood itself as standing within the historically continuous drama of God's self disclosure . . . that runs from Abraham through Moses and the prophets to Jesus and the Christian church."[3] As the church traced its legacy to Israel, it developed an understanding of history.

History: two approaches.—Two distinct approaches to history are evident in the religion and culture of ancient civilizations. These are known as *cyclical* and *linear* history. In the cyclical view, history is conceived as an unending cycle of rise and decline, moving toward no purposeful end. Societies begin, flourish, and collapse only to be replaced by other civilizations which follow the same inevitable course. History mirrors the seasonal pattern of life, death, and rebirth. If God does exist, He is to be discovered beyond the unending cycle of history. Knowledge of God is discovered outside the cycle, beyond history and time. The cyclical view of history is characteristic of ancient Zoroastrian and Babylonian religion, as well as Buddhism and Hinduism. It is essentially a pessimistic approach to history and the human dilemma. The task of religion is to help persons escape the "circle" of history in order to discover reality.

For both Judaism and Christianity, history is perceived, not as an unending, meaningless cycle but as a continuum, a line begun by God moving toward a mysterious but purposeful end. While God is transcendent, above and beyond history, he is also immanent, revealing Himself in the course of human events. The Author of history has chosen to intervene in history.

This so-called linear view of history was a distinct element of Hebrew faith from the beginning. The renowned British historian Herbert Butterfield said, "The God who brought his people out of the land of Egypt, out of the house of bondage, was to be celebrated in the Old Testament pre-eminently as the God of history."[4] The words, "In the beginning God" (Gen. 1:1), testify to divine activity in creation, time, and space. In the covenant with Abraham, the deliverance from Egypt, the giving of the law at Sinai, and other historic events, the Hebrews charted God's direct intervention in their history. Generation after generation remembered Egypt, the Red Sea, Sinai, and Canaan. Israel recalled, "They cried to the Lord in their trouble and he delivered them from their distress" (Ps. 107:6).

The "Church" in Israel

In those historic events a community was born, the *laos tou theou,* the people of God. It was a community formed by God Himself. "I will take you for my people, and I will be your God" (Ex. 6:7). The people of God, therefore, appeared in history long before the incarnation of Jesus Christ. As Paul Minear wrote, "The early Christians did not date the beginnings of God's people from Jesus' birth or ministry . . . or even from the descent of the Spirit at Pentecost, but from the covenant-making activity of God in the times of Abraham and Moses."[5] In Israel, God chose a people as His own. He revealed Himself to and through this dynamic community, a community given to spiritual insight and willful disobedience. As the people of God, Israel was more than a nation, it was a community of faith. The history of Israel details the struggle of the people of God to understand and fulfill their calling.

For the early Christians, the community begun in Israel had been radically expanded in the church. The linear movement of history extended from creation through the covenants with Abraham and Moses to Jesus of Nazareth (Acts 3:13). The church was the new people of God, not separate from but grafted into the tree of Israel (Rom. 11:17). "But you are a chosen race, a royal priesthood, a holy nation, God's own people. . . . Once you were no people, but now you are God's people" (1 Pet. 2:9-10).

The early church saw itself as descended from that "great . . . cloud of witnesses" who had experienced God's presence and anticipated a fuller revelation which was to come (Heb. 11:1 to 12:2) In a sense, those faithful believers represented a "church" before Jesus, a community which lived in hope of the Promised One. The New Testament writers did not hesitate to speak of those earlier Jewish "saints" in Christians terms. The writer of Hebrews suggested that Moses "considered abuse suffered *for the Christ* greater wealth than the treasures of Egypt" (Heb. 11:26, author's italics). Hebrews also indicates that the historic faith of Israel "should not be made perfect" apart from Christ and His church (v. 39). In understanding itself as the people of God, the early church secured a powerful historical identity in the past, a sense of continuity in the present, and a prophetic consciousness toward the future.[6]

A Covenant People

To suggest that God is active in human history means that He discloses Himself in word and deed within the framework of time and space. Revelation, therefore, is the means by which God makes Himself known to humanity. Both Israel and the early church insisted that God's action in history was not chance or arbitrary, but purposeful and relational. God was not casually involved in human affairs, but intervened in the lives of individuals throughout history. He revealed Himself to human beings and sought to have relationships with them. One important sign of that relationship was the covenant. A covenant is simply an agreement or contract by which two groups or parties agree to relate to each other.

The covenant which God made with Israel involved several elements. It began with God. The Creator chose to enter into relationship with His creation. Likewise, the covenant was built upon historical events—the promise to Abraham, the deliverance from Egypt, and the giving of the law at Sinai. It was a covenant which required a faithful response from the people of God. At the same time, it was a covenant which revealed the grace of God. God chose a people, not because of their faithfulness, but because of His love. The covenant was given "because the Lord loves you, and is keeping the oath which he swore to your fathers, that the Lord has brought you out with a mighty hand, and redeemed you from the house of bondage" (Deut. 7:8).[7]

The Church and the Covenant

Like Israel, the early Christians thought of themselves as God's covenant people. The New Testament writers saw the church as both an heir of the covenant with Abraham and the fulfillment of that new covenant anticipated by the prophet Jeremiah in which God would put His law "upon their hearts" (Jer. 31:31-34). So, Paul wrote, "Our sufficiency is from God, who has qualified us to be ministers of a new covenant, not in a written code, but in the Spirit" (2 Cor. 3:5-6, author's translation). As the covenants with Abraham and Moses brought new life to Israel, so the covenant in Christ brought new life to the whole world. Through Christ's death and resurrection, the covenant was both renewed and transformed. Christ was "the mediator of a new covenant" (Heb. 9:15a), as well as the fulfillment of the old (Gal. 3:23-29).[8]

The Signs of the Covenant

The newness of the covenant in Christ was evident in those "signs" of the covenant which developed in the church. As heirs of the old covenant, the early Christians did not carelessly discard the ancient covenantal signs but extended their meaning to new symbols. As Israel recalled God's historic activity in particular observances and events—circumcision, Passover, sabbath, and assorted festivals—so the church established symbols which reminded them of the new covenant in Christ.

Baptism.—In the church, the Jewish practice of proselyte baptism was extended to all believers and invested with new meaning. In baptism, new believers "put on Christ" (Gal. 3:27) and, as Paul wrote, "If you are Christ's, then you are Abraham's offspring, heirs according to promise" (v. 29).

Worship.—The new communities which gathered for prayer and praise clearly followed the model of the synagogue, with one dramatic addition: They proclaimed Jesus of Nazareth as the resurrected Christ of God. Wherever they gathered in His name Christ was present (Acts 2:46).

The Supper.—As the Passover meal assured Israel of its covenant relationship with God, so the Lord's Supper was the continuing sign of the church's covenant. In it the people of God both remembered and experienced the presence of Christ anew. Through the supper, the church affirmed its unity with Christ and with one another (1 Cor. 10:16-17).

Yet as significant as these symbols might be, Christ Himself is the ultimate sign of the new covenant. Christ was the "paschal lamb" who had been sacrificed (1 Cor. 5:7). The blood of the lamb, which in the old covenant had spared Israel, in the new covenant secures the salvation of the world (Eph 1:7). Christ Himself is the covenantal sign.

The Presence of the Logos

For the early Christians, Christ was the bridge between the covenants, old and new. He was the link which united the church with God's earlier revelation of Himself. The idea of the logos was one way in which the New Testament writers sought to describe Christ's activity. For many ancient religions and philosophies, the logos was a "life force" or inner principle which was the source of insight and wisdom about God and the individual.[9] For Christians, the Word (Logos) of God which became flesh in Jesus was that timeless presence which mediated the will of God to humanity. As John's Gospel declares, "In the beginning was the Word and the Word, was with God, and the Word was God" (1:1). We call this the doctrine of Christ's preexistence. It is the belief that the same Christ who is the source of the church's faith is also the agent of God's activity throughout history. As the new communities of faith sought to explain what Jesus meant, not only to their time but to all times, they proclaimed His preexistence.

In Colossians 1:15-18 Paul wrote that the same Christ who is head of the church is the source of all creation.

> He is the image of the invisible God, the first-born of all creation; for in him all things were created, in heaven and on earth, visible and invisible, whether thrones or dominions or principalities or authorities—all things were created through him and for him. He is before all things, and in him all things hold together. He is the head of the body, the church.

Christ is the agent of both creation and redemption. "Christ is the mediator of the new creation, the redeemer from death and bondage, the creator of the new community of 'new beings.'"[10]

By implication, therefore, the church which began in the "fulness of time" with Jesus of Nazareth was present throughout history in the timeless Word of God. As the New Testament writers searched for the presence of Christ in the history of creation and salvation, they also looked for traces of His church.

Paul himself described Israel's wilderness experience as if it were a church. Those ancient events, Paul believed, paralleled the church's own historic experience. The Israelites, Paul said, were "baptized into Moses in the cloud and in the sea, and all ate the same supernatural food and all drank the same supernatural drink. For they drank from the supernatural Rock which followed them, and the Rock was Christ" (1 Cor. 10:2-4). Even without realizing it, Israel experienced the presence of Christ in those events which one day would be clearly identified with His new people, the church (1 Pet. 1:10-11).

Preexistence, thought not a biblical term, is the biblical way of uniting the faith of the church with the faith of Israel, a faith grounded in God's historic acts from creation to covenant to the incarnation. The Word (Logos) by which the church was begun was the Word by which the world was made. Creation, redemption, and church are all bound together by the Word of God. That Word, revealed throughout history, was made flesh in Jesus Christ.

The Church and the Incarnation

Jesus Christ, the head of the church, is the incarnate Son of God. For Christians, the incarnation of Jesus Christ is the most significant event in human history. Through the incarnation, the God who revealed Himself in history entered history itself. As the Nicene Creed declares:

> One Lord Jesus Christ, only begotten Son of God, Begotten of the Father before all the ages, Light of Light, true God of true God, . . . who for us . . . and our salvation came down from the heavens, and was made flesh of the Holy Spirit and the Virgin Mary, and became man, and was crucified for us.[11]

As the incarnation informs our understanding of the nature of Christ, it also informs our understanding of the nature of the church. Indeed, the church must continually examine its identity and ministry in light of the incarnation. What does the incarnation reveal about Jesus and His church?

Begotten of the Father

Sent from God.—The incarnation suggests that Jesus Christ, the church's founder, is the incarnate Son of God, "the only begotten of the

Father" (John 1:14, KJV; compare 3:16). Jesus was not merely another religious teacher, prophet, or miracle worker. He was not simply another god to be included in the world's museum of deities. He is the incarnate Son of the eternal Father. "God was in Christ, reconciling the world to himself" (2 Cor. 5:19, KJV). Jesus did not come into the world alone. He was the one whom God had promised and in whom God dwelt (Col. 1:19-20; 2:9).

Through Christ, therefore, the church is united to God the Father. So Jesus admonished His disciples, "In that day you will know that I am in my Father, and you in me, and I in you" (John 14:20). Those who have received Christ, have received the Father also. "If a man loves me," Jesus said, "he will keep my word, and my Father will love him, and we will come to him and make our home with him" (v. 23).

Sent on mission.—As the Father's only begotten Son, Jesus was sent into the world for a specific purpose. It was a mission at once simple and profound: "For God so loved the world that he gave his only Son, that whosoever believes in him should not perish but have eternal life" (John 3:16). The incarnation involved a unique person with a unique mission. "The Father sent the Son to be the Saviour of the world" (1 John 4:14, KJV).

The church, therefore, understands its own mission in light of Christ's mission. The church's mission comes from the Father through the Son. As the church proclaims the mission and message of the Son, it does the will of the Father.

Revealing the Father.—Through the incarnation of God's only begotten Son, the church understands more clearly the nature of God Himself. "He who has seen me has seen the Father," Jesus said (John 14:9). The fullest self-disclosure of the Father is found in His only begotten Son. As the church experiences the life of the Son, it becomes more closely related to the Father. As it proclaims the gospel of the Son, it reveals the nature of the Father to the world. The incarnation of God's only begotten reveals some important, often surprising, characteristics of God the Father. He is the God who humbles Himself and becomes of no reputation (Phil 2:7-8). He is also *abba* who comes to His people as Father (Matt. 6:9). In the humility, gentleness, servanthood, and suffering of Christ, we discover something of the nature of the Father. As Fisher

Humphreys wrote, "The qualities which characterize Christ also characterize God."[12] Thus the church's understanding of God is judged in light of the nature of Christ.

The Word Became Flesh

"The Word became flesh, and dwelt among us, (and we beheld his glory, the glory of the only begotten of the Father,) full of grace and truth" (John 1:14, KJV). Jesus Christ is not merely begotten of the Father, He is Himself the very Word of God. What is the Word of God? In its most basic sense, the Word of God is God's revelation of Himself to humanity. In terms of Christian faith, the Word of God is the presence of Christ coming to us. Those two truths were united in the incarnation. Through the incarnation, God revealed Himself in the person of Jesus Christ. The faith of the church is built on the person of Jesus Christ who is the incarnate Word of the living God. J. Robert Nelson wrote, "To say that Jesus Christ, in his earthly human life, in His death, in His risen life is the divine Word, above all other forms of it, is simply to restate the primary proposition of the Christian faith."[13] When the church proclaims that the Word became flesh, it declares that God communicates beyond the partial disclosures of law or dogma. Through the incarnation, God revealed Himself distinctly in Jesus Christ.[14] The Word of God to which the New Testament testifies was experienced first by the church in the life of Jesus Christ. The early Christians bore witness to "that which was from the beginning, which we have heard, which we have seen with our eyes, which we have looked upon and touched with our hands, concerning the word of life" (1 John 1:1).

Yet the church does not simply proclaim that the Word of God became flesh in Jesus Christ. It must also declare what the Word means in human history. So the life, death, and resurrection of Christ provides the verification of God's self-revelation in Jesus. He who became flesh lived, died, and rose again. In those events God was truly "in Christ, reconciling the world to himself." An English Methodist confession provides a summary: "The Word of God thus interpreted as Christ Himself, living on earth, crucified, risen; Christ Himself as preached; Christ Himself as revealed in the pages of the Scriptures—this Word of God calls the church into existence and perpetually sustains it."[15]

The Promise of the Spirit

The promise of the Spirit provides the means by which the church experiences the Word of God (Christ) beyond the event of the incarnation. In the Gospels, particularly John's Gospel, Jesus continually pointed to the Spirit as the one who would "guide you into all the truth" (John 16:12).

We cannot discuss the relationship of the church to the incarnation apart from the promise of the Spirit. Without that promise, the incarnation is limited to the historic moment of the earthly life of Jesus. Through the Spirit, Christ is experienced in every age. The church is not only sustained by the memory of Christ's incarnation as an historic event but also experiences the continuing presence of Christ through the Spirit. As Jesus Himself declared, the Spirit "who proceeds from the Father, he will bear witness to me" (John 15:26).

The promise of the Spirit is closely linked to the incarnation. John the Baptizer declared, "I have baptized you with water; but he will baptize you with the Holy Spirit" (Mark 1:8). Indeed, Jesus Himself reminded His followers that it was imperative that He go away from them in order that the "Comforter" might come to continue His work (John 16:7-11, KJV). "The Spirit is thus the earthly presence of the glorified Lord. In the Spirit Christ becomes Lord of his Church and in the Spirit the resurrected Lord acts both in the community and in the individual."[16]

The Church: An Incarnate Community

Through the Holy Spirit, the church lives in the light of the incarnation. The promise of the Spirit is a call to continue the work of the incarnate Lord. Jesus said, "He who believes in me will also do the works that I do; and greater works than these will he do, because I go to the Father" (John 14:12).

The incarnation of Jesus Christ was truly a unique event which can never be repeated. "For Christ also died for sins once for all, the righteous for the unrighteous" (1 Pet. 3:18). He is the only begotten Son of God whose presence in the flesh accomplished what no other could accomplish.

As the body of Christ, however, the church is called to continue Christ's work in the world. That fact has led numerous individuals to suggest that the church somehow represents the continuation of Christ's incarnation. As the body of Christ, the church extends the incarnation to each new age. The Word continues to take on flesh through the church on earth. Thus the church, which originates in the incarnation, becomes the means for extending that event throughout history.

To suggest that the church is the continuation of Christ's incarnation is perhaps to claim too much for the church. While Christ is the foundation of the church, He is also beyond the church. The church is not more than Christ but Christ is more than the church. The church is a divinely ordained community, but it is not divine. The Word became flesh only once in Jesus of Nazareth.

Perhaps it is best to speak of the church as an incarnate community of those who have received the Word of God in Christ Jesus and seek to incarnate that Word in their own lives through the power of the Holy Spirit. To such an incarnate community, Paul wrote, "Let this mind be in you, which was also in Christ Jesus" (Phil. 2:5, KJV); "Christ in you, the hope of glory" (Col. 1:27); "Yet not I, but Christ liveth in me" (Gal. 2:20, KJV); and "For me to live is Christ" (Phil. 1:21). Unlike its Lord, the church's experience of divine life is always partial and incomplete. It awaits the fullness of the kingdom when wholeness is experienced entirely (1 Cor. 13:12). As the incarnate community, the church is not an end in itself but points always to Christ, the incarnate Son of God. As Christians live out the gospel, they continue to express the Word of God in flesh. As they respond to concrete human need, they continue the incarnate work of Christ. They make His love to be seen in human lives.

The Church in Jesus' Teaching

The Word became flesh in Jesus Christ. The four Gospels—Matthew, Mark, Luke, and John—provide accounts of Jesus' life and teaching with particular attention to His crucifixion and resurrection. The church is ever dependent on the Gospel material for insight into its identity, mission, and message.

What did Jesus Himself say about the church? Very little, if we count only His two brief references to the church as recorded in Matthew's Gospel (Matt. 16:18; 18:17). A great deal, if we understand that the nature of the church is shaped irrevocably by the life and teaching of its Lord as revealed in the Gospels.

The Beginnings of the Church

Did Jesus intend to found a church? When did the church begin? Those two questions have received a variety of answers in the history of the church.

At one end of the spectrum are those who suggest that Jesus was the founder of a particular ecclesiastical organization, which became the Roman Catholic Church. Its foundation was established by Christ's declaration (Matt. 16:18) to Peter that "on this rock I will build my church." Peter is the rock on which the church is built. Peter and his historic successors, the bishops of Rome, possess the power of "the keys of the kingdom" with authority in heaven and earth (Matt. 16:19). All of Jesus' teaching in the Gospels is to be understood in light of these verses and their relationship to a particular institution, the church, as founded on the apostles, bishops, and popes.

At the other end of the spectrum is the idea that Jesus came to preach the kingdom of God, not to found the church. This approach, popularized in this century by the Catholic "modernist," Alfred Loisy, suggests that "Jesus proclaimed the Kingdom of God, and what came was the church."[17] This view denies that Jesus in any way envisioned an elaborate organization or institution which would carry on His work. The church was established by Jesus' followers when the kingdom of God did not appear. Between these two extremes are other more moderate interpretations of Jesus' intent for the community of believers which followed Him.

R. N. Flew insightfully observed that Jesus' teachings provide the church with no elaborately developed theological structure or ecclesiastical system. Rather, the church in the Gospels is "a new community, with a new way of life, a fresh and startling message, and unparalleled consciousness of inheriting the divine promises made to Israel."[18] The church begins, not with organizational structure, but with the life to which Jesus calls His new community. Jesus provided His followers with a "task to fulfill" rather than precise instructions for organizing a church.[19] Like those first followers, we are drawn to the church primarily by the life of Jesus. His teaching in the Gospels provides the seed which grows toward maturity through the guidance of the Holy Spirit.

Many Beginnings

When did the church begin? It is impossible to establish a precise moment. Perhaps it is best to say that the church had many beginnings. It began with persons and events. In a sense, the church began with the covenant people, Israel, long before Jesus Christ entered human history. The newness of the kingdom as taught by Jesus is always understood in relationship to the old order which it fulfills.

Jesus was not merely the founder of a new religion nor the creator of another religious institution. He is the Redeemer—the fulfillment of that community of faithful people long present in the world. "Think not that I am come to destroy the law, or the prophets: I am come not to destroy, but to fulfil" (Matt. 5:17, KJV).

In another sense, the church began with the incarnation. The community begun in Israel became a new community with the coming of Jesus Christ. The very appearance of God in the flesh marks a new beginning for the people of God. Yet Jesus' appearance in history is inseparable from His activity in history. The church began, not merely with an incarnational event, but in the entire activity of Jesus' incarnate life. Every facet of Jesus' ministry—His calling of the twelve, His ethical teaching, His response to sinners and outcasts, His crucifixion and resurrection—represents a new beginning for the church. The church began both at Christmas and at Easter.

Pentecost, another of those beginnings, marked the confirmation of Jesus' life and teaching as the church experienced the Spirit of the resurrected Christ. At Pentecost the community called out by Jesus was empowered to continue Christ's ministry and message in the world.

The church had many beginnings. It began in Israel with the covenant people, with the incarnation of Jesus Christ, with the calling of the twelve and the teaching ministry of Jesus. It began at the cross and in the triumph of Jesus' resurrection. It began at Pentecost in the powerful experience of the Holy Spirit. Perhaps it begins in each new age as persons discover the community of faith for themselves. The church's origins lie not in one specific event but "in the whole action of God in Jesus Christ."[20]

A Community of Disciples

The church which began with Jesus took shape in that community of disciples which first gathered around Him. Initially, they did not see themselves as members of an organization or an institution but as learners who sought to follow Jesus and be instructed by Him. In those early disciples, the church was born. Through them we discover some basic aspects of the church in the teachings of Jesus.

A Special Group of Followers

The community of disciples was a specific group of persons who responded to Jesus' call and followed Him. The twelve apostles occupied a particularly significant place in Jesus' life and ministry (Matt. 10:1-4). They received intensive instruction and were His closest confidants. They were the first to be sent forth with the good news of the kingdom (11:1). They were the first to recognize Him as the promised Messiah (16:13-20). To them He explained the teachings which the "multitudes" did not understand (13:10-17). Yet in spite of their intimacy with Jesus, the apostles did not fully comprehend His mission or His message (16:21-23).

With the resurrection and the experience at Pentecost, the apostles became the leaders of the church. Their teaching and witness provided authoritative guidance for the new communities of faith.

The apostles were not the only disciples whom Jesus called, however. There were numerous men and women who constituted the broader community of Jesus' followers. They also received His teaching and became the mainstay of the early church. They are represented in the women who also followed (Luke 8:2-3) and in the seventy who were also sent out with the message of the kingdom (10:1-20). They were among those who gathered in the upper room in anticipation of the advent of the Holy Spirit (Acts 2:1-4).

A Consciousness of a New Era

Early believers were conscious that they belonged to a new era, although they were uncertain as to what it meant and where it would lead (John 14:22; Mark 13:4). Many had left "everything" behind when they became a part of this community of disciples (Mark 10:28).

Instructions for a Specific Mission

The disciples received particular instructions from Jesus for a specific mission. They, like their Lord, were to declare the immediacy of the kingdom. It was a task so urgent that they were not to develop elaborate programs or organizations or give extensive attention to basic physical needs (Matt. 10:5-15). Thus "when the day of Pentecost was fully come" (Acts 2:1, KJV), the disciples simply continued in what they had already been taught, though, no doubt, with new power. They not only preached the kingdom but also proclaimed Jesus as the risen Lord (Acts 2:22-24). The church began with those first disciples. Their calling and sacrifice constituted the heart of the church's call to discipleship. It is a model for those who continue to follow Jesus.

A New Symbol of Fellowship and Community

To that group of disciples Jesus gave a new symbol of fellowship and community, the Lord's Supper. In that event, shared on the evening before His death, Jesus led them from the Passover of the old covenant to the "communion" of the new. At the table of the Lord, the disciples discovered a powerful symbol of their unity with their Lord and with one another. The teachings of Jesus do not provide elaborate organizational or institutional instructions for the church. They demonstrate a dynamic life and message which must constantly inform the life of the church however it is expressed.

The Gospel of the Church

The gospel of the redemption which Jesus proclaimed became the gospel of the church. For Jesus, the gospel was simply the good news that the long-awaited kingdom (Mark 1:15) was at hand.[21] While the gospel was built upon the promises of God to Israel, it also created a new Israel, restored and reconstituted. The gospel message which Jesus proclaimed was the gospel which the church itself was called to declare. What was the nature of the gospel which the church received from Jesus?

A Vision of the Kingdom of God

Jesus gave the church a vision of the kingdom of God. It was the kingdom which He preached. The kingdom was not established by political intrigue or military power but by spiritual life. It represented the "reign of God" in the hearts and lives of men and women. The life of the gospel, therefore, anticipated the life of the kingdom.

A New Relationship with God

The church also received from Jesus a gospel of a new relationship with God. God was the source of the kingdom, and He alone would create it. Jesus instructed the new community to pray, "Thy kingdom come, Thy will be done" (Matt. 6:10; Luke 11:2). Yet the God of the kingdom was also *abba*, Father, who had revealed Himself in His only Son.

A New Relationship with Others

The gospel of Jesus provided the church with a new relationship with others. The citizens of the kingdom are those who turn the other cheek, go the extra mile, and love their neighbors as themselves (Matt. 5:38-48). Their gospel contains an all-inclusive love and a forgiveness without limits. It is a gospel which reaches out to the outcast and the dispossessed. It is good news to the poor, the victimized, and the broken-hearted (Luke 4:18-19).

A Missionary Gospel

The gospel which Jesus gave to the church is a missionary gospel. Those who have heard and accepted the gospel are the "sent ones" who do not keep the news to themselves but spread the word in the world (Matt. 28:19-20). The gospel which began with a remnant is God's word of salvation for all. The people who follow Jesus are to make known the good news.

Good News of Jesus Himself

The church receives the good news not merely *from* Jesus but *of* Jesus Himself. Each of the four Gospels ends with an account of the crucifixion and resurrection of the Christ. These events are inseparable from the life and teaching of Jesus. The early Christians believed that without them there was no gospel (1 Cor 15:14-20). Christians preached not only Christ's kingdom and ethical precepts and religious teaching but also Christ Himself and "him crucified" (1 Cor. 2:2). The church cannot receive the gospel of Jesus apart from Jesus Himself as the crucified, risen Lord.

Jesus and the Church

Without Christ there is no church. Jesus is the source of the church's life and the foundation of its hope. "In him we live and move, and have our being" (Acts 17:28). The church not only teaches about Jesus but also proclaims Jesus Himself. It looks to Jesus in order to discover its identity and mission. The church must extend Jesus' teaching and mirror Jesus' life in the world.

Savior of the Church

"Christ loved the church," Paul wrote, "and gave himself for it" (Eph. 5:25). Jesus is the Savior of the church. He is the Good Shepherd who "lays down his life for the sheep" (John 10:11; compare v. 15), Jesus does not simply organize the church which bears His name, He saves it. The church is not only the messenger of the good news, it is the recipient of it. In fact, the church must never forget that it too has a Savior. It is forever in need of grace. The church can only declare the salvation it has received.

Thus the community of faith, like the individual believer, understands its salvation in light of the saving work of Christ, His life, crucifixion, and resurrection (Eph. 1:17). Indeed, Paul insisted that the church itself is reconciled into one body "through the cross" (2:16). To be Christ's, the church must stand "under the cross."[22] Without the cross and the resurrection, the church has no gospel and no reason for being (1 Cor. 15:14-20). The church is the community of the cross. The community of faith may offer salvation only because it has been saved. It may speak of forgiveness because it has been forgiven and of love because it has known the love of Christ (Rom. 8:1-2, 31-39). The Lord of the church is also the Savior of the church, who offers Himself "as a ransom for many" (Matt. 20:28).

Servant of the Church

Christ who saves the church, serves the church. He "emptied himself," Paul declared, taking "the form of a servant." Christ "humbled himself and became obedient unto death" (Phil. 2:7-8). Jesus' death on the cross was the culmination of His role as servant to His people. The cross event was not some mechanical transaction but the ultimate expression of a life of servanthood. It is a manner of life evident throughout the Gospels. We observe it in Jesus' association with the outcasts of His society, in His response to the hungry, the sick, and the disabled; and in His willingness to take the servant's role with His disciples (John 13:1-11). Jesus' teaching on self-sacrifice is verified by the servanthood which He demonstrated in His own life. "[For] the Son of man came not to be served, but to serve" (Matt. 20:28). He was, the church believes, the very personification of that Suffering Servant foretold by the prophet Isaiah (Isa. 53:1-12).

In the Gospels, Jesus' life of servanthood is often contrasted with the self-serving attitudes of His disciples. They were frequently more concerned about preserving their own status than fulfilling their calling in the world (Luke 22:24-30). Like the earliest disciples, the church often ignores the servanthood of Jesus and its implications for the community of faith. Yet Jesus Himself remains the servant of His church.

Model for the Church

Jesus, the servant, is the model for the life and ministry of the church. The church which is served by Jesus is called to serve in His name. Jesus not only practiced servanthood but also extended that calling to those who would follow Him. In fact, servanthood is the most basic characteristic of those who are citizens of the kingdom. "Whoever would be first among you must be your slave" (Matt. 20:27). Those whose feet are washed by Jesus must learn to wash the feet of others. "For I have given you an example that you also should do as I have done to you" (John 13:15). Jesus is the example, the model, for the church's life and ministry.

Being Christian is no easy calling. In fact, the church's history illustrates the tendency of God's people to spiritualize, rationalize, or otherwise ignore Christ as the true model for its identity. Like the first disciples, the church in every age is ever learning who Christ is, what His gospel means, and how it is to be applied. The church often fails miserably in conforming to the image of Christ. Perhaps the humility of Jesus is the church's greatest attribute as it seeks to live in light of One who "made himself of no reputation" (see Phil. 2:5-8, KJV).

On one hand, Jesus has given us an example of what we are to be and do. Jesus, the servant, has created a community called to servanthood. The gospel commands that those who follow Him be conformed to His image (Rom. 8:29). But this community is also a community of sinners who need the grace of Christ to follow Him and carry out His commands. Such a reality creates a continuing struggle for the church. The church which seeks to follow the model of Christ is the same church which falls short of its calling and needs the grace of its Savior to overcome.

Head of the Church

The church looks to Jesus for its life, its teaching, and as its model for ministry. Thus this chapter ends where it began, with the assertion that Jesus Christ is head of the church. The church is Christ's body, and He is head of that body. The church draws its entire life from Him. In every age the church seeks to conform to His image. Apart from Christ there is no church. He is not only the source of the church's authority; He is the source of its very life.

Notes

1. Jürgen Moltmann, *The Church in the Power of the Holy Spirit* (New York: Harper and Row Publishers, 1977), p. 66.

2. Robert S. Paul, *The Church in Search of Itself* (Grand Rapids: Wm. B. Eerdmans Publishing Co., 1972), p. 283.

3. E. Clinton Garner, *The Church as a Prophetic Community* (Philadelphia: The Westminster Press, 1967), p. 102.

4. Herbert Butterfield, *Christianity and History* (New York: Charles Scribner's Sons, 1960), p. 9.

5. Paul S. Minear, *Images of the Church in the New Testament* (Philadelphia: The Westminster Press, 1960), pp. 70-71.

6. Robert Nelson, *The Realm of Redemption* (Greenwich, Conn.: The Seabury Press, 1951), pp. 18-19.

7. Howard Grimes, *The Christian Views of History* (Nashville: Abingdon Press, 1969), p. 55.

8. Ibid., pp. 58-60.

9. Fred Craddock, *The Pre-Existence of Christ in the New Testament* (Nashville: Abingdon, 1968), pp. 11-80.

10. Ibid., p. 88.

11. "The 'Nicene' Creed," *Documents of the Christian Church*, Henry Bettensen, ed. (New York: Oxford University Press, 1963), pp. 36-37.

12. Fisher Humphries, *The Nature of God*, "Layman's Library of Christian Doctrine"(Nashville: Broadman Press, 1985), 4:55.

13. Nelson, p. 106.

14. Ibid., p. 103.

15. Ibid., p. 115.

16. Hans Küng, *The Church* (New York: Sheed and Ward, 1967), p. 166.

17. Ibid.

18. R. Newton Flew, *Jesus and His Church* (London: Epworth Press, 1949), p. 18.

19. Nelson, p. 22.

20. Küng, p. 76.

21. Ernest F. Scott, *The Nature of the Early Church* (New York: Charles Scribner's Sons, 1941), p. 32.

22. Moltmann, p. 97.

3

The Church as New Testament Community

The church of Jesus Christ is a New Testament community. Its identity is shaped by the New Testament church and the New Testament Scriptures. The New Testament church occupied a particular time and place in human history, but it remains a timeless spiritual community which provides an enduring witness to the essential nature of the church. The way in which the primitive Christian communities experienced and communicated the Word of God continues to inform the church of its identity. While the contemporary church can never repeat the historical context of the first century, it must seek to understand its mission in light of the revelation evident within the New Testament communities. That revelation is transmitted to the church by the Holy Spirit through the Holy Scriptures. The Scriptures are our link to the New Testament church. In every age the church is called to be a New Testament community, living in the light of those great ideals revealed to the first generation of Christians.

The Church and the Scriptures

Holy Scripture is the church's witness to the revelation of God in Jesus Christ. Yet the Bible is not the Word of God because the church declares it so but because the Bible brings an authentic Word of God to the church.[1] The church of New Testament times became a New Testament community as it experienced and proclaimed the Word of God. As first-century Christians were inspired to write about those experiences and that proclamation, the New Testament was born. Thus we may say that the church produced the New Testament and the New Testament produced the church. The church is both a response to the Word of God and a vehicle of that Word. The Scriptures are the authoritative Word of God

37

for the church. Through the written Word (Scripture), the Living Word (Christ) is manifested in the power of the Holy Spirit.

The Question of Authority

Every human community—familial or tribal, political or religious—must be organized around some authority which serves as a guide for corporate life. Through its sources of authority, a community understands its identity and judges its actions. The question of authority has been a significant issue for the church from its beginning. By what authority does the church function in the world? By what authority should the life of the church be evaluated? What are the authoritative teachings of the church?

From the earliest times, Christians have insisted that Jesus Christ, the living Word of God, is the ultimate authority for the church. The life of the believer and the life of the church are subject to Jesus' authority in all things (Col. 1:18). During Jesus' early ministry, His life and teaching provided an immediately authoritative source for the community of disciples which gathered around Him. When he had gone away from them into heaven (see Acts 1:11), however, the church faced a new dilemma regarding the authoritative knowledge of the Word of God. In their quest for authority, the early Christians turned to several sources, among them the leadership of the apostles, the guidance of the Holy Spirit, and the authority of Holy Scriptures.

Apostolic authority provided a major source of direction for the early church. The apostles were recognized as having particular authority due to their closeness with Jesus and the teaching which they had received from Him. The significance of the apostolic authority can be seen in Paul's struggle to establish his own apostolic credentials within the skeptical Christian communities (2 Cor. 11:1 to 12:21). The apostles (Paul included) charted the course of the early church and were authoritative witness to the church's calling under God.

The presence of the Holy Spirit in the community of faith was also a major source of authority for the early church. Jesus had promised that this authoritative resource would follow Him and lead the believers "into all the truth" (John 16:13). Thus the early church was a community highly sensitive to the movement of the Spirit.

Paul suggested that leadership in the church was to be carried out by certain "charismatic" (spirit-filled) individuals who exercised particular gifts within the community of faith. These leaders—apostles, prophets, evangelists, pastors, and teachers—exercised their particular gifts, providing authoritative direction for the fledgling communities (Eph 4:11; 1 Cor. 12:28). This dependence on the Spirit was not without dangers, however. Some tried to manipulate the power of the Spirit for their own selfish ends (Acts 8:18-24). Others challenged apostolic authority (Paul's, for example) by claiming an authority of their own (2 Cor. 11:13-15).

As the church grew and the apostles died, the question of authority became increasingly complex. When the apostles were gone, who would represent the final authority in the church? How would church conflicts be resolved? How would truth be distinguished from error? In response to those challenges, the church turned increasingly to the Scriptures of the Old and New Covenants as an authoritative witness and guide to divine authority.

The Church's Use of Scripture

The Old Testament

From the beginning, Scripture served as a major source of authority for the church. The Hebrew Scriptures constituted the church's first Bible. Jesus appealed to the Scriptures as the authoritative basis for His own ministry and mission (Luke 4:16-21). The early Christian preachers grounded their proclamation in the Word of God to Israel and their belief that Jesus was the fulfillment of that Word (Acts 2:14-36).

The earliest Christian writers of the second century used Old Testament texts as authoritative guides for the early Christian communities. Even as the use of New Testament materials became more prominent, most Christians continued to revere the Old Testament as divinely inspired authority for the church. As we have already noted, the church tended to "Christianize" much of the Old Testament, reading its prophecies and precepts in the light of Christ. In this effort the early Christians employed particular methods such as typology and allegory. Through typology the church viewed Old Testament texts and persons as "types" which represented and anticipated Christian events. So the flood was a type of baptism, the ark a type of church, and Moses a type of Christ.[2]

Through allegory the early Christians interpreted Old Testament texts as "symbols . . . of spiritual truths."[3]

The New Testament

As the church developed its own identity outside the boundaries of Old Testament Judaism, it looked to the authority of those distinctively Christian Scriptures which formed a "New Testament." These writings both shaped and were shaped by the life of the early Christian communities. Increasingly, first-century Christian worship incorporated readings from the Hebrew Scripture (usually in its Greek translation called the Septuagint) and the growing collection of Christian writings which were circulated throughout the churches. These materials provided information, edification, and spiritual direction for the fledgling Christian communities. They became the authoritative Word of God to the church.

The earliest New Testament writing came from the apostle Paul. Written over a twenty-year period beginning around AD 48, Paul's Epistles represent an authoritative response to issues which confront the church in every age. They also form the earliest Christian theology as Paul described what it means to be "in Christ."[4] The Gospels—Matthew, Mark, Luke, and John—were essential witnesses to selected events in the life of Jesus. Other later writings, such as Hebrews, James, 1, 2, and 3 John, 1 and 2 Peter, Jude, and the Revelation, were also read extensively in the churches. They provided authoritative guides to Christ and His will for both the individual and the community.

The Development of the Canon

The books which now make up the New Testament were not the only ones read and revered in the first-century churches, however. Other writings appeared alongside the biblical materials. These included such works as the *Didache,* a handbook of church order and discipline, and the Shepherd of Hermas, a popular and highly apocalyptic writing. As the apostles died, the churches grew, and the number of "sacred" writings increased, the church sought to distinguish those books which were uniquely inspired and, therefore, authoritative for the community of faith. The development of a canon, or list of authoritative Scriptures, was a significant task for the early church.

Three primary criteria seemed to have been involved in determining the inspiration of specific materials. The first criterion involved apostolicity. That is, did the book reflect apostolic authorship or apostolic association? Was the author an apostle or an associate of the apostles? Second, a widespread acceptance in the churches was required. Was there general agreement in the churches to the book's authority? Third, the contents of the book were to be edifying for the churches. In other words, did they bear the witness of the Spirit in the life of the community?[5] Some materials, such as the Gospels and Paul's Epistles, were common to every list. Less immediate agreement occurred with books like Hebrews, where apostolic authorship was not readily evident. Likewise, the highly apocalyptic nature of the Book of Revelation made it questionable in some churches.

The earliest canon grew out of a major controversy within the church. As early as AD 144 an intense and devout preacher named Marcion attempted to purge Christianity of all its Jewish influences. He believed that the Old Testament contained an inferior revelation which was unworthy of the truth of Christ. For Marcion, the Old Testament God was a cruel deity whose harsh religion could not be reconciled with the God of love personified in Jesus Christ. He dismissed the Old Testament completely and developed a list of New Testament books composed primarily of the one Gentile Gospel, Luke, and Paul's Epistles. Marcion's actions compelled the church to develop its own list of inspired books more precisely. While the canon as we now know it was not formally recognized until the fourth century, "the *idea* of a canon was accepted and the apostolic writings were regarded as the main source of doctrine."[6] The church, therefore, exists in the Scripture and the Scripture informs the continuing life of the church.

The Church in the New Testament

The church not only reads the Scriptures as an authoritative Word of God but also exists within the Scriptures themselves. The church of the New Testament is an authoritative witness to the nature of the church in all times. Therefore, the models and life of the New Testament churches inform the continuing life of the church of Jesus Christ.

Words Define the Nature of the Church

As the church looks to the Scriptures for an understanding of its nature, it turns to specific words which the New Testament writers used in
describing the Christian community. While specific words are used for
the church in the New Testament, they provide only a beginning for our
understanding of the biblical nature of the church. Beyond the words are
the images which the biblical writers also use to define the nature of
Christ's church. The two best-known words which the New Testament
uses for church are: *ekklēsia* and *koinōnia*.

Ekklēsia.—When the New Testament writers referred to the church,
they used the word *ekklēsia* more than any other. That word appears
some one hundred twelve times in the New Testament. When the Old
Testament was translated into Greek (Septuagint), the word *ekklēsia* was
used for the Hebrew word *qahal*. In Hebrew, *qahal* means "to call out"
and is used to describe the community or assembly of God's faithful
people. In Judeo-Christian thought, *qahal* and *ekklēsia* involve not *an*
assembly, (Neh. 13:1) but *the* assembly of God.[7] In 1 Kings 8:14, for
example, *ekklēsia* is the assembly of those who gather together in the
name of God. Like Israel, the New Testament *ekklēsia* is made up of
those whom God has called out. Unlike Israel, it is composed of those
who have been called out *by Christ*. While related to God's earlier assembly, Israel, the new *ekklēsia* is a uniquely Christian society. It is the
church, the assembly of Christ.[8] In using the word *ekklēsia*, the New
Testament writers suggested that the church was the new community
growing out of the old. *Ekklēsia* was less an elaborate institution or organization than a living organism of persons united to Christ and one another.[9] By definition, *ekklēsia* requires community. The church as
ekklēsia is a visible community of faith.

Because the word *ekklēsia* refers primarily to local congregations,
some have concluded that the church itself is known only in its local
form, that each congregation is "independent" of the other. The New
Testament *ekklēsia* was a visible community of believers which exercised
significant local distinctiveness, even autonomy, but was in no way spiritually independent of other Christian congregations. Extreme individualism obscures the intent of other New Testament ideas and images
regarding the nature of the church. While *ekklēsia* is a valuable concept

for understanding the New Testament church, it is inseparable from another New Testament word, *koinōnia*.

Koinōnia.—If *ekklēsia* describes the community of the church, *koinōnia* describes the nature of that community. New Testament writers used the word in various ways. Paul's writings illustrate this diversity.

In two passages (2 Cor. 13:14 and Phil. 2:1), Paul referred to the *koinōnia* of the Holy Spirit. In 1 Corinthians 1:9 he declared that Christians have *koinōnia* with the Father and the Son. In Romans 15:26 and 2 Corinthians 8:4, he used the word in reference to an offering for those in need; and in 1 Corinthians 10:16-17, Paul united the idea of *koinōnia* with the sharing of the bread and the cup at the supper. In Acts 2:42, *koinōnia* is utilized to describe one of the significant elements of the church after Pentecost. "They devoted themselves to the apostles' teaching and fellowship *(koinōnia)*, to the breaking of bread and the prayers."[10]

While contemporary Christianity has frequently used the English word *fellowship* to define *koinōnia,* the meaning is much deeper than the casual associations or get togethers which that word often describes. In its New Testament usage, *koinōnia* means "to share in," "to have communion with," "to be involved in partnership together." The relationship which characterizes *koinōnia* is closely related to that of covenant, involving a dual partnership with God and with other persons. *Koinōnia* begins in relationship with God and extends to all those who have relationship with him.[11] The community of the church is based on the common union which Christians share with Christ. The church, therefore, is a spiritual *koinōnia* gathered around Jesus Christ, sharing in His presence.[12]

Paul said this *koinōnia* is experienced in a particularly powerful way at the Lord's table. The supper is *koinōnia* (communion), a means of sharing in Christ's presence together (1 Cor. 10:16-17).

Spiritual *koinōnia* is also expressed in relationships within the body of Christ. As Paul collected an offering for the desperate church at Jerusalem, he used the word *koinōnia*. The *koinōnia* was the offering (Rom. 15:26; 2 Cor. 8:4), a real means of communion.[13]

Koinōnia is a nonnegotiable characteristic of Christ's church. The church is a communion of persons who share a relationship with Christ and with one another. The love which is received from Christ must be offered to others. Without that, there is no church. This *koinōnia* cannot be maintained selectively. It is not limited to geographic, racial, social, or economic class but permeates the whole church. Selective *koinōnia* is unworthy of the communion of the saints.

The word *koinōnia* has numerous uses in Holy Scripture. Yet each usage points to the central factor: relationship with God and with other persons. There is no church, no *koinōnia,* apart from relationship.[14]

Images Describe the Nature of the Church

The Biblical Use of Images

The nature of the church is not just described in specific words—*ekklēsia* or *koinōnia*. It is also developed in Scripture through the use of powerful images. It is not enough to examine those words which the New Testament uses to define the church. The New Testament use of such terms as "People of God" or "Body of Christ" also describe the nature of the church. Each image calls us to creative and lively ways of understanding the church. Avery Dulles wrote that biblical images "suggest attitudes and courses of action; they intensify confidence and devotion. To some extent they are self-fulfilling; they make the church become what they suggest the church is."[15]

What is an image? In one sense, an image is a word picture. Images provide a broader definition of the church than individual words could ever accomplish. Images produce mental pictures of what the church is and should be. The use of images for describing the nature of the church was no haphazard choice on the part of biblical writers. Many grew out of older images which were reinterpreted in light of the incarnation of Jesus Christ, that is, (people of God); others (that is, body of Christ), were developed as a particularly Christian imagery.[16]

Images are word pictures which help us understand our relationship to the church of Jesus Christ. The New Testament writers used many images to describe the nature of the church. One image or word was not enough. The church is not just the people of God; it is also the body of Christ. No one image captures the total identity of the church. Each image informs and completes another. Together, they create a composite picture of the nature of the church. In his classic study, *Images of the Church in the New Testament,* Paul Minear said that a conservative estimate of the New Testament images for the church would number between eighty and one hundred different pictures. He listed several "minor" images which include "the salt of the earth," (Matt. 5:13); "A Letter from Christ," (2 Cor. 3:2-3); "Fish and Fish Net" (Mark 1:17; Matt. 4:19); "The Boat" (Matt. 8:23-27), and many others.[17] Obviously, we cannot examine all of the biblical images here. We must concentrate on the certain selected images which illustrate the diverse pictures of the church which the New Testament produced.

People of God

We have already seen that the idea of the people of God is an image which spans both Testaments, Old and New. The people of God existed long before the church. Yet the New Testament writers were quick to point out that the church had become God's new people. In Galatians, Paul insisted that faith in Christ, not circumcision or conformity to the law, incorporated an individual into the people of God (Gal. 3:1-7). In the Corinthian letters, Paul warned that God's new people should learn from Israel's experience of divine judgment. Though they had received a fuller revelation of God, the new people had to be faithful to that vision lest they too face judgment (1 Cor. 10:1-13). We may conclude that these passages mean: "You are God's people (2 Cor. 6:16), therefore you must live as God's people (2 Cor. 6:17) in order to be God's people"[18] (2 Cor. 6:18). To be God's people is to live as God's people. While the church boldly asserts its identity as the people of God, that identity is not grounds for arrogance or pride, but humility, discipleship, and spiritual growth.

The image, people of God, should provide great security for the church and the Christian. It links the church with all God's faithful people throughout time and provides an identity in the divine scheme of things. "Once you were no people but now you are God's people; once you had not received mercy but now you have received mercy" (1 Pet. 2:10). As God's people, the church is to be "built into a spiritual house, to be a holy priesthood, to offer spiritual sacrifices acceptable to God through Jesus Christ"[19] (1 Pet. 2:5).

Body of Christ

Through the image body of Christ, the New Testament describes that which makes the new people of God unique. They are in Christ; they belong to Him; they are part of His body, the church. Indeed, the term *body of Christ* is one of the most significant New Testament images for understanding the nature of the church (Rom. 12:5; 1 Cor. 12:27; Eph. 4:12).

The idea of body (sōma) *is a significant image in both the New Testament world and the New Testament itself.*—In Hebrew thought, body was a link to peoplehood. So certain individuals could be used to represent in themselves the whole human family. The first Adam, for example, represented in himself the corporate personality of all humanity. When Paul wrote, "in Adam all die," he was referring to Adam as a representative of the whole human race (Rom. 5:12-21). The Suffering Servant described in Isaiah 53 bore the iniquities of a whole people.[20] Likewise, first-century Greek thought viewed the world as one body of which humanity was one part.

The Gospel writers pointed to the significance of Christ's body at the Last Supper and the crucifixion. Jesus described His own body as the source of salvation around which the church is gathered. The New Testament image of the body of Christ unites the Hebrew idea of corporate relationship with the Greek concept of body as a unity of various parts.[21] As the body of Christ, the church involves the whole people of God brought together in Christ.

The image, body of Christ, helps define the church's identity in significant ways.—First the church does not represent the body of Christ, it *is* the body of Christ. The body of Christ is Christ Himself in direct and intimate relationship with His people. It is Christ's own presence in the life of His church. As Dale Moody wrote, "This does not mean that the church is Christ, but it does mean that there can be no true church apart from vital union of the members with Christ."[22]

Second, the image, body of Christ, involves an essential and inescapable unity. The church is not part of the *bodies* of Christ but the *body* of its Lord. Paul stressed this unity in the image of a body incorporating many parts: "For just as the body is one and has many members, and all the members of the body, though many, are one body, so it is with Christ" (1 Cor. 12:12). The church is bound to Christ. There is no relationship to the church apart from Him. Therefore, all who are united to Christ are united to one another. The church is not merely a group of individuals who occasionally meet together. Its members are a body intimately united to Christ and each other. Within this unity, there is a rich diversity of participants and functions. Because Christians are already one body united to Christ, they ought to live as one body in Him.[23]

Third, Christ is the Head of His body, the church (Col. 1:18; Eph. 1:22-23). There are many parts of the body, made up of a diversity of persons, but only Christ is or can be the head. He alone maintains a distinct relationship to the whole church. As head He has a unique place and function in the church. The church is the body of Christ, but it has not yet achieved the wholeness of Christ who remains its head. (Eph. 4:13). Christ's headship gives unity, purpose, and direction to the body.[24] Because of the faithfulness and completeness of the head, members of the body, though incomplete, remain within the body of Christ.

Some of Paul's most profound statements on the nature of Christ's body and relationships within that body were written to Corinth, one of the most fragmented of the New Testament communities. The Corinthian church, though sinful, remained a part of the body of Christ. Paul's concern was that the Corinthians live according to that spiritual reality.

Finally, two of the most significant "signs" of incorporation into Christ's body are baptism and the Lord's Supper. (1 Cor. 12:13; 10:16-17). The significance of those events for the church will be discussed later in this volume.

Household of Faith

The images of people of God or body of Christ stress the communal identity of the church. This identity is made clearer in the image of the church as the household of faith. The community of the church is the community of a family. As with other images, the understanding of the new family, the church, is informed by the old family, Israel. Abraham was called to be the "father" of a chosen race, the "children" of Israel (Gen. 17:5-8). As a covenant people, the Jews were related to God and one another as a family among the nations. In them "all the families of the earth" would be blessed (Gen. 28:14; Rom. 4:16-17). For the Hebrews, the concept of family was the foundation of all forms of community.[25]

Through Jesus Christ, the church represents a new family (household) bound together, not by flesh and blood, but by faith. In using this image, the New Testament writers united the church with that most basic element of human society. Although the term "household of faith" or "household of God" appears only occasionally in the New Testament (Gal. 6:10; Eph. 2:19), the image it conveys is evident throughout.

The image of family involves a new understanding of the parental relationship between God and His people.—The church is composed of those who know God as *abba*, Father and Parent (Rom. 8:15; Gal. 4:6-7). Those who have this relationship with God are justly called the "children of God" with all the benefits and inheritance of heirs (Rom. 8:16-17).

Membership in the family has been extended from Israel to those who were once "far off" from God.—In fact, those who were once illegitimate (Gentiles) are now incorporated into God's family in Christ (Rom. 9:30-33; 11:17-19; Eph. 2:13). The image of the children of God has been expanded beyond Israel to all those who believe. "For ye are all the children of God by faith in Christ Jesus" (Gal. 3:26, KJV).

As members of the household, believers become sisters and brothers in relationship with one another.—The evidence of love for God and participation in the family is revealed in the relationship which the children of God maintain with each other (1 John 3:1-24; 4:20-21). "By this it may be seen who are the children of God, and who are the children of the devil: whoever does not do right is not of God, nor he who does not love his brother" (1 John 3:10). Thus, not all belong to the household, only those who live in faith and love.

Personal faith carries with it familial implications. Conversion and membership in the church brings an individual into a family which shares common joys and sorrows (Rom. 12:15). It is also a family with the potential for disagreement, conflict, and sin. Family life in Christ demands continuing maturity as the whole church moves toward conformity to its elder brother, Jesus Christ.

Communion of Saints

While the specific phrase, "communion of saints," is not found in the New Testament, the idea of the church as "communion" *(koinōnia)* and as "saints" *(hagios)* is clearly present in Holy Scripture. Thus the image of the church as a communion of saints becomes an important concept for understanding the church in the New Testament. We have already seen that *koinōnia* involves the idea of a close-knit, intimate community.

The word *saint (hagios)* clarifies the nature of that community. The word is used over one hundred times in eighteen different New Testament books. The New Testament writers did not always use the term *saints* synonymously with *church,* yet in numerous instances a reference to "the saints" is the same as a reference to "the church" (John 17:17-19; Acts 9:31-32; Heb. 2:10-12; 1 Pet. 2:9-10; Jude 3; Rev. 20:9).[26]

In the New Testament, saints are not an elite group of persons selected for their spiritual superiority, but the whole body of Christian people. Paul wrote, "To all God's beloved in Rome, who are called to be saints" (Rom. 1:7). Again, he addressed a letter, "To all the saints in Christ Jesus who are at Philippi" (Phil. 1:1). Saints are all those who have faith in God through Jesus Christ. The church is a community of saints.

The word *saint (hagios)* describes the nature of the Christian life, not merely for a few, but for everyone. Saintliness involves holiness, a holiness which comes from God and in which the church shares. Saints are persons who have been sanctified (made holy) by the Spirit and who are seeking to incorporate more of that holiness into their daily lives. The goal of the saints is holiness. God said, "You shall be holy, for I am holy" (1 Pet. 1:16). As the church preaches, teaches, witnesses, and worships, it contributes to the continued holiness of the saints. As the saints live according to the life of the Spirit, they contribute to the holiness of the church. Saintliness is a gift the believers receive as a quality of life which they must pursue each day.

The communion of the saints also means that the church pursues holiness in community. In most New Testament references, the word *saint* is expressed in the plural. Sanctification is a corporate experience. No one is made holy apart from the community of faith, the communion of saints.[27] The saints share in the sanctifying power of the Holy Spirit.

Fellowship of the Holy Spirit

Whatever else the church may be, it must be a fellowship of the Holy Spirit. As Paul Minear observed, "Wherever the church is spoken of as the saints, the power of the Holy Spirit is assumed to be at work within it."[28] Where there is no Spirit, there is no fellowship *(koinōnia)*. Where there is no *koinōnia,* there is no church. Through the Holy Spirit, the church moves from being simply another organization of people to a "spiritual fellowship" intimately related to Jesus Christ and one another

(1 Pet. 2:5). Although the image "fellowship of the Spirit" is used precisely in only two New Testament passages (2 Cor. 13:14; Phil. 2:1), the concept unifies other images to provide "the very essence of the church."[29] The *ekklēsia* is a *koinōnia* in the Holy Spirit. The gifts by which the community fulfills its mission are secured in and through the Spirit.

What does the image, "fellowship of the Spirit," mean to the nature of the church? First, it means that God Himself is the author of the fellowship. No one can acknowledge that Jesus is Lord except through the Holy Spirit (1 Cor. 12:3). Second, the Spirit frees the church to live according to the gospel. "For the law of the Spirit of life in Christ Jesus has set [you] free from the law of sin and death" (Rom. 8:2). Third, the Spirit provides the gifts which contribute to the fellowship. The *gift* of the Holy Spirit makes possible the *gifts* of the Spirit within the church (1 Cor. 1:7; Rom. 1:6; Eph. 4:11).[30] Fourth, the fellowship experienced in worship is the work of the Holy Spirit (Acts 2:42-47). There is no true Christian worship without the Spirit's presence. Fifth, the unity of the fellowship is the work of the Holy Spirit (Eph. 4:2-7). The church is the creation of the Holy Spirit. As the church gathers, it does so with a faithful recognition that the Spirit is present.

The fellowship of the Spirit is that image which unites all images. Through the Spirit, the church continues its ministry. These images can help the contemporary church evaluate its own life as a New Testament community. The life of the New Testament church in the Spirit informs our understanding of what it means to be a New Testament church in the present day.

The Life of the New Testament Churches

Words and images are not the only means for understanding the nature of the church in the New Testament. The life of the New Testament church—practices, attitudes, and controversies—define its identity in every age. The Scriptures declare the essential unity of the church within the diverse life of the New Testament churches. From the Book of Acts to the Book of Revelation, the New Testament materials describe or respond to particular issues in the lives of the specific churches.

The Acts of the Apostles, for example, provides some of the most extensive information about the life and practices of the early church immediately after Pentecost. It was a church guided by the Holy Spirit through the apostles. Its members shared "all things in common," worshiping in the Temple as well as in "the breaking of bread and the prayers." The church preached the gospel and baptized in the name of Jesus Christ. It was consumed by a missionary vision for presenting the gospel throughout the world. It was a persecuted church which soon experienced its first martyrdom. It was also a community in which abuses took place, where falsehood and avarice occurred. Through it all, however, the church in Acts lived in the light of the Holy Spirit's power.

Likewise, Paul's Epistles reflect the life and struggles of the earliest churches outside Jerusalem. Some churches, like Philippi, were strong and mature. Others, like Corinth, were immature and fragmented. Still others, such as Galatia, were confronted by divisive theological controversies.

Each of the books addresses significant issues in the first-century churches which inform the continuing life of the entire church. The churches confronted questions related to morality, personal and corporate. They struggled with their relationship to the state and to other religions. They examined the implications of the gospel for sexuality, family life, and the nurture of children. They developed ideas regarding the nature of Christian faith for the new convert and the mature disciple.

The church in the New Testament is at once a timeless witness to the nature of the church for all times and a reminder that the church can never be completely divorced from its historical setting. Every church lives in the light of the New Testament community. But the historical context of the church influences the way its members interpret the meaning of the New Testament church for themselves.

There is no doubt that the New Testament church is a model for the church's continuing identity. All Christian traditions, no doubt, consider themselves to be valid New Testament churches in one form or another. Roman Catholics, Eastern Orthodox, and Anglicans point to their apostolic succession of bishops as evidence of their link with the New Testament. Baptists and Disciples of Christ see believers baptism by immersion as evidence of the New Testament church. Pentecostals claim to have discovered the same outpouring of the Holy Spirit as the New Testament church experienced at Pentecost. Episcopalians, Presbyterians, and Congregationalists believe their form of church government to be the closest to the New Testament norm. Which tradition represents the "true" New Testament church? The fact is, in terms of practice and function, there probably was not one single New Testament church model but numerous New Testament models.

In one sense, the life of the New Testament churches was unique and unrepeatable because those communities were the first to experience new creation in Christ. Yet the New Testament church is also a timeless witness to and for the church in every era of human history. For the church must always revaluate itself in light of its origins. When the church becomes too worldly, too conformed to the principalities and powers of this present age, it is called to return to the vision of its beginning, a vision which even the original New Testament church did not fully make use of. In the midst of great diversity, the New Testament churches were unified in their calling to be conformed to the image of Christ whose body they were. It is not enough, therefore, merely to repeat the practices of the church as described in the New Testament. New Testament churches in any age are those which conform to the image of Christ through the presence of the Holy Spirit within the community of faith.

Notes

1. Robert Nelson, *The Realm of Redemption* (Greenwich, Conn.: The Seabury Press, 1951), pp. 109-111.

2. J. N. D. Kelly, *Early Christian Doctrines,* rev. ed. (New York: Harper and Row Publishers, 1978), pp. 69-72.

3. Ibid., p. 70.

4. J. G. Davies, *The Early Christian Church* (Garden City, N.Y.: Anchor Books, 1967), p. 10.

5. Ibid., p. 114.

6. Ibid.

7. R. W. Kicklighter, "The Origin of the Church," *What Is the Church?* Duke McCall, ed. (Nashville: Broadman Press, 1958), pp. 30-31.

8. Jürgen Moltmann, *The Church in the Power of the Holy Spirit* (New York: Harper and Row, Publishers, 1977), pp. 317-318.

9. Kicklighter, p. 40.

10. Nelson, p. 53.

11. Ernest F. Scott, *The Nature of the Early Church* (New York: Charles Scribner's Sons, 1941), pp. 152-153.

12. E. Clinton Gardner, *The Church as a Prophetic Community* (Philadelphia: The Westminster Press, 1967), pp. 48-50.

13. Kicklighter, pp. 38-40.

14. Nelson, pp. 56-57, citing L. S. Thornton, *The Common Life of the Body* (London: n.p., 1942), p. 76.

15. Avery Dulles, *Models of the Church* (Garden City, N.Y.: Image Books, 1978), p. 25.

16. Paul S. Minear, *Images of the Church in the New Testament* (Philadelphia: The Westminster Press, 1960), p. 17.

17. Ibid., pp. 28-65.

18. Hans Küng, *The Church* (New York: Sheed and Ward, 1967), pp. 121-122.

19. E. Glenn Hinson, *The Integrity of the Church* (Nashville: Broadman Press, 1978), p. 48.

20. Dale Moody, "The Nature of the Church," in McCall, ed., p. 21.

21. Eduard Schweizer, *The Church as the Body of Christ* (Richmond: John Knox, 1964), pp. 13-22.

22. Moody, p. 22.

23. Küng, p. 229.

24. Nelson, pp. 80, 95.

25. Minear, p. 166.

26. Ibid., p. 136.

27. Wallace Alston, Jr. *The Church* (Atlanta: John Knox, 1984), pp. 37-42.

28. Minear, p. 137.

29. Moody, p. 25.

30. Ibid., p. 27.

4

The Church as Evangelist-Teacher

"Go therefore and make disciples of all nations, baptizing them in the name of the Father and of the Son and of the Holy Spirit, teaching them to observe all that I have commanded you; and lo, I am with you always, to the close of the age" (Matt. 28:19-20). In that brief passage, sometimes known as the Great Commission, the church discovered a powerful directive for its mission in the world. The church is an evangel, telling the story of Jesus, making disciples throughout "all [the] nations." The church is also a teacher, instructing Jesus' disciples in the life of the gospel. Evangelization and instruction are inseparable elements of the total mission of Christ and His church.

From the beginning of His own ministry, Jesus identified Himself as an evangel, one who announces good news. In the synagogue at Nazareth, He declared, "The Spirit of the Lord is upon me because he has anointed me to preach good news to the poor. . . . to proclaim release to the captives, . . . to set at liberty those who are oppressed, to proclaim the acceptable year of the Lord" (Luke 4:18-19). Wherever He went, Jesus preached the gospel of the kingdom and commanded His followers to do the same (Matt. 9:35; 10:7).

Jesus was also a teacher, instructing multitudes and individuals in the nature of the kingdom life. Matthew's Gospel says that "when Jesus had made an end of commanding his twelve disciples, he departed thence to teach and to preach in their cities" (11:1, KJV). The church, like its Lord, is an evangel-teacher. Preaching and teaching are distinct yet interrelated expressions of the same gospel. Indeed, each contains elements of the other. When the church evangelizes, it also teaches; when it teaches, it also evangelizes. Each calling is necessary to the fulfillment of the gospel. The church cannot fulfill its calling unless both elements—evangelism and teaching—permeate its life.

Evangelism and Teaching

A Teaching Evangel

The church is an evangel, a herald of good news. Yet, even as it tells the story, it teaches the faith. The gospel is not the possession of a privileged few but is to be spread abroad for all to hear. The gospel is Jesus; He is the source of the good news. Michael Green wrote that the early preachers of the good news "had one subject and one only, Jesus."[1] The New Testament preachers told the story of Jesus in order to bring persons to Jesus Himself. The good news is not merely *about* Jesus, it *is* Jesus, known in the power of the Spirit. He is the *euaggelion*, the gospel. As the church proclaims Jesus, it proclaims the good news.

The New Testament uses several words to describe the church's evangelical task, each closely related to the other. *Euaggelion* means simply the good news. Originally it referred to those specific events which brought salvation and the "act of announcing them."[2] *Kērugma* is the word for "proclamation." It is the declaration that the good news has occurred. *Martureō* is the Greek word translated "witness." It describes one who had firsthand experience of the risen Christ. Michael Green united all three words in a basic statement of Christian evangelism: "The gospel is good news; it is proclamation; it is witness."[3]

In his classic work, *The Apostolic Preaching and Its Development*, published in 1936, C. H. Dodd suggested that the *kērugma* (proclamation) of the early church contained six clearly discernable points, evident in New Testament preaching. The early preachers declared that:

1. The Age of fulfillment has come.
2. It has been accomplished through the life, death, and resurrection of Jesus.
3. Through the resurrection, Jesus is exalted to God's right hand as the Messiah of the new Israel.
4. The presence of the Holy Spirit in the church is evidence of Christ's continuing power and glory.
5. The messianic age will soon reach its consummation in Christ's return.

  6. The *kērugma* concludes with a call for repentance, the promise of
     forgiveness and salvation for those who enter the "elect commu-
     nity."[4]

Many other scholars insist that the content of New Testament *kērugma*
(proclamation) was less uniform than Dodd suggested. They show that
the early Christian preachers used considerable "versatility" in their
preaching, stressing various aspects of the same gospel story. All agree,
however, that the goal of such preaching was faith in Christ, the Savior of
the world[5] (1 Cor. 1:17-24).

As the early Christians preached the good news, they also taught the
faith. The content of Christian preaching, however elementary, provided
instruction in the basic elements of the gospel. Through the *kērugma,* the
church called persons to salvation and taught them the way in which
salvation could be secured. "Repent and be baptized," Peter admonished
his hearers on the day of Pentecost (Acts 2:38). It was a word of both
proclamation and instruction. As the apostles proclaimed the gospel,
they taught others. Those who heard and believed also declared what
they had seen and heard.

As the gospel was preached, the church was born. The dynamic power
of the *kērugma* helped to create the *ecclēsia*. The idea of the church itself
was contained within the *kērugma*. "The word of God increased, and the
number of the disciples multiplied in Jerusalem" (Acts 6:7).[6] The church
gathers around the proclamation of the gospel, and the church is gathered as the gospel is proclaimed.

The church can never relinquish its evangelical calling. The story of
Jesus must be told and retold in every age. The gospel which the church
preaches is the same gospel it teaches.

An Evangelical Teacher

The church is a teacher, instructing persons in the nature of Christian
faith and discipleship. It is called not only to "make disciples" but also to
teach them to follow the way of Christ (Matt. 28:19). The faith which the
kērugma proclaims must be nurtured and undergirded by the *didachē*,
the teaching ministry of the church.

The importance of the church's teaching ministry is evident throughout the New Testament. The apostles received extensive instruction directly from Jesus. The early Christians "devoted themselves to the

apostles' teaching and . . . prayers" (Acts 2:42). Paul's letters were written primarily to churches and Christians who required continued instruction in the faith. Indeed, Paul asserted that the apostles, prophets, pastor/teachers, evangelists, and other church leaders work together "to equip the saints for the work of ministry, for building up the body of Christ, until we all attain to the unity of the faith and of the knowledge of the Son of God" (Eph. 4:13). Instruction, therefore, enables Christians to "grow up in every way unto him who is the head, into Christ" (v. 15). The content of the church's teaching reflects the diversity of the church's life.

The church presents basic information about Jesus and His mission in the world.—The preaching of the early evangelists always contained elementary details of Jesus' life ("he went about doing good"), His death ("whom they slew and hanged on a tree"), and His resurrection ("God raised him up the third day") (Acts 10:38-41, KJV).

The four Gospels were written to provide some account of the life and teachings of Jesus as "a declaration of those things which are most surely believed among us" (Luke 1:1, KJV). The earliest creeds were concise statements of essential elements of the faith, easily memorized by new converts. As the gospel was extended to the Gentiles, the church's instructional task became more complex. Those outside the Judaic tradition lacked even rudimentary knowledge of the faith and required extensive instruction.

By the third century, these *catechumen* (learners) were required to receive instruction for up to three years before being admitted to the church. Candidates for baptism were instructed in doctrine, ethics, and liturgy (worship). Their behavior and life-style was monitored as evidence of their commitment to Christ and His church. Later, these teachings were written down in catechism books, manuals for instruction in faith and doctrine. Martin Luther's Shorter Catechism remains in use in Lutheran churches. The Westminster Catechism of 1648 was a significant Presbyterian manual of doctrinal instruction. James P. Boyce, Southern Baptist theologian and preacher, also wrote a Baptist catechism for the instruction of young people. Boyce wrote that the aim of such books was "to bring the truth taught within the comprehension of children of ten to twelve years old and upwards."[7] It was a means of preparing the young for faith.

The modern church faces an equally challenging task of teaching the gospel to persons reared in an increasingly secular culture. Contemporary Christians cannot presuppose even basic knowledge of the Bible or the faith. Persons, young and old, should be instructed in Christian doctrine and practice before and after baptism. The church is constantly retelling the story of Jesus in its most basic form. Perhaps Evangelical Christians should rediscover the catechism as a means for teaching Christian faith.

The church instructs its members in Christian spirituality.— Christians should not remain "babes in Christ" but grow in the "grace and knowledge" of the Lord (1 Cor. 3:1-3; 2 Pet. 3:18). That process of spiritual growth and maturity is what we mean by Christian spirituality, "the practice of the presence of God" in the life of the individual. Spirituality does not come easily or immediately. It must be taught, cultivated, and experienced. As teacher, the church identifies the "gifts of the spirit," the attributes of faith, and the means for experiencing God's grace. The church is a spiritual guide, aiding its members in the discovery of spiritual gifts and maturity in faith.

The church provides instruction in ethics.—C. H. Dodd commented that in the New Testament "teaching *(didaskein)* is in a large majority of cases ethical instruction."[8] While ethical demands are central to the gospel, the church does not promote ethical requirements as an end in themselves. Ethical instruction is not a new legalism but a reflection of Christ's new commandment to love one another (John 13:34-35). His command to love represents a higher law which distinguishes Jesus' followers from others in the world (Rom. 8:13). The ethical standard taught by the church contains both individual and communal implications. Like its New Testament counterpart, the modern church instructs its members in truthfulness, fidelity, stewardship, and other aspects of personal conduct. It also teaches concern for the poor and the oppressed, the hungry and dispossessed. The church itself is judged by the same ethics it teaches. Every issue is evaluated in light of Christ, the supreme ethical teacher and example for the church.

The church teaches Christian doctrine.—It instructs the community in the basic essential truths of the faith so that its members may not be "tossed to and fro, and carried about by every wind of doctrine, by the sleight of men, and cunning craftiness" (Eph. 4:14, KJV). The church has a responsibility to help its members distinguish between those doctrines and prophets which are true and false.

Yet the doctrine which the church teaches is not an end in itself. Like all the church's instruction, the end of all doctrinal teaching is Christ. He is the one doctrine by which all others are judged.

As the church teaches, it also evangelizes. It provides a witness to the truth of the gospel. As Christians live according to the gospel, as they practice the faith in daily living, they provide a witness to gospel faith. Evangelism is not merely "telling out" the good news. It is also "living out" the truth of Christ day by day.

Evangelizing and Teaching Children

Instruction and evangelization are two inseparable elements of the one gospel. Both are involved in the conversion of persons to Christian faith. The church does not simply teach those who already believe. It also instructs persons who are on the way to faith. Sometimes the church teaches persons before it evangelizes them. Nowhere is this more evident than in the Christian nurture of children. Since the second generation of Christians appeared on the scene, teaching and nurture have been an essential part of the church's evangelism. Paul's words to Timothy—"I am reminded of your sincere faith, a faith that dwelt first in your grandmother Lois and your mother Eunice" (2 Tim. 1:5)—imply that Timothy may well have been taught the faith before he believed it. As the church teaches children, it prepares them for the gift of the gospel.

The contemporary church must reassert its role as evangelical teacher, unashamedly affirming the demands and doctrines of the faith. It must gently nurture children and exemplify a Christianity which will lead them to make faith their own.

The Mission of the Church

The church is a missionary community. Preaching and teaching are the means by which the church fulfills its mission: to make known the reconciling love of God. Mission is an inescapable element of the church's life. All Christians are called to participate in the mission of the church. All are ambassadors who represent Christ in bringing the gospel to all persons (2 Cor. 5:20).

The one mission of the church is carried out through many missions—

specific programs of missionary outreach, local, regional, and international. Yet the Christian mission is not merely something which occurs "over there" or "with those people" through the work of specialized, official missionaries. It is the redemptive activity of the whole people of God expressed in multiple forms. Mission is the "whole church in action."[9] When the people of God minister in Christ's name, wherever they are, they fulfill the mission of the church.

Witness to the World

The church is on mission in the world. Though called out from the world, the church exists in the world as a witness to the love of Christ. It accepts the world as the arena of God's creative and redemptive activity, while recognizing the dangers of "worldliness" in its own life.

In the New Testament, the term for witness, *martureō,* means to testify, to give evidence of firsthand experience or knowledge. The New Testament Christians bore witness to God's love in word and deed. They declared the gospel at every opportunity—in palaces and in prisons, to rich and poor, in acceptance and rejection. They were witnesses to faith even in the face of death. Indeed, the Greek word for *martyr* is another form of the word *witness.*[10]

Yet the church is not just a community of individuals who witness to their personal faith. The church itself is a witness. Its entire ministry is a testimony to the power and reality of the spiritual life. The church is a sign to the world of the activity of God. As a witness, the church is both prophet and servant. As prophet, it brings a word of judgment on the sins and superficiality of society. Its life of sacrifice should provide a contrast to the selfishness and exploitation which often characterize human relationships. The church is witness to the value of human life. It lives in the light of the "Lamb of God, who takes away the sin of the world" (John 1:29). This prophetic witness sometimes brings persecution and repression (ask Christians in totalitarian regimes), but it is an inescapable element of the church's mission.

The witness of the church is also found in servanthood. Like its Lord, the church takes the "form of a servant," feeding the hungry, clothing the naked, caring for the sick and imprisoned (Phil. 2:7; Matt. 25:31-46). The New Testament uses the word *diakonos,* less to define an official group in the church than to describe the servant role of the community of faith. It is a service which Jesus Himself exemplified and to which He called His disciples (John 13:1-17).

The church's service extends even to those who reject and repudiate its witness. The church's most Christlike witness is evident in love and service to its enemies.

Servanthood is not something which follows witness; servanthood is witness. Indeed, E. Glenn Hinson wrote that the church's witness is found in "pouring out its life to satisfy human need wherever and in whatever form it finds it." Self-sacrifice, not self-protection, is the heart of the church's mission.[11] Somehow in recent times, the distinction between the church as witness and the church as servant has been greatly exaggerated. Divisiveness occurred over the "true" mission of the church. Some said it was evangelism—direct witness to the power of the gospel. Others said it was social service—direct response to the needs of humanity. The fact is, there is no "true" gospel apart from both those elements of Christian witness. Neither can exist without the other. The church declares its witness as it evangelizes and serves those in need. This is the "full gospel" which seeks to lead persons to wholeness.

Wholeness in the Faith

The church has a twofold mission: to take the gospel to those who do not yet believe and to instruct and encourage those who do. The church is a witness to the need for faith. It is also a witness to the wholeness which faith can bring. The church's ultimate goal is to guide persons to wholeness, to become "new creations" in Christ Jesus (2 Cor. 5:17).

When the gospel overtakes us, it transforms us into new creations; but we remain "earthen vessels" given to fragility, vulnerability, and sin (2 Cor. 4:7). The entrance into faith does not provide instant wholeness. It offers the promise of wholeness which is to come, while providing the grace to live and work toward wholeness along the way. The way to wholeness is a long and tedious process (1 Cor. 13:12). "Christians are made, not born," the third-century theologian Tertullian wrote. By that he meant that Christian discipleship is a lifelong process. The church provides a community in which wholeness may be nurtured and where brokenness may be cared for. In so doing, it offers consolation to those who grieve, forgiveness to those who have sinned, and reconciliation for those who have strayed.

This ministry of reconciliation and wholeness is offered in community. Wholeness is not merely the church's goal for particular individuals, it is the aim of the entire people of God. Because the church is the body of Christ, brokenness in any member affects the entire body. The hope of the kingdom is toward a day when all the members of Christ's body are made whole (Isa. 35:1-6; Rom. 8:22-24). Perhaps the church's wholeness is best exemplified by its response to the most broken people in its midst. So the church must reach out to those whose lack of wholeness is most evident—the outcast, the oppressed, the handicapped, and the disfranchised. If the promise of wholeness does not extend to the most needy, it cannot apply to anyone.

As an instrument of the Holy Spirit, the church fulfills its witness through preaching, teaching, worship, and the "cure of souls." As Carlyle Marney wrote: "The church is a womb where God's kind of persons happen, are made, are called forth."[12]

The Church and Salvation

The church proclaims salvation through Jesus Christ. It instructs its members in the meaning of salvation and provides a community in which the gifts of salvation may be experienced. Yet what is the relationship of the church to the nature of salvation itself? In what way does the church participate in the process of salvation?

One ancient response to that question is found in the Latin phrase, *extra ecclesiam nulla salus,* "outside the church there is no salvation." This idea was prominent in the writings of many leaders of the early church. Cyprian, the third-century bishop of Carthage, wrote, "He can no longer have God for his Father, who has not the Church for a mother."[13] In other words, to be outside the church is to be outside Christ. Such a view originated in the early church's effort to respond to persecution from without and heresy from within. It was based on an idea that the correct doctrine of salvation could only be found in that one body which alone possessed orthodox teaching and divine authority. By the Middle Ages, the doctrine became increasingly associated with the claims of the Roman Catholic Church that only in its fellowship was salvation secured. Thus to be cut off from the institutional church was to be cut off from Christ and salvation.

The Protestant Reformers rejected such a concept, stressing that faith alone was the sole requirement for salvation. There was no salvation outside Christ and whoever was united to Him was united to the church. With time, however, this emphasis on the individual nature of salvation and increased disillusionment with the church led many people to reject the need for any institutional or organizational form of religion. The structures and teachings of the institutional church were viewed as hindrances to genuine faith. In many contemporary gatherings, secular and religious, the easiest way to enliven the crowd is to attack the institution of the church. Some modern preachers have turned the ancient confession around to suggest that there may not be much salvation in the church at all. Salvation is a private matter and participation in the church is, at best, one of many options for the saved.

To say that there is no salvation outside the church is to say too much. To say that the church is unrelated to salvation is to say too little. Both extremes go too far. The idea of no salvation outside the church fosters a narrow view of salvation and an elitist understanding of the church's mission. Yet the isolation of modern religious individualism denies the need for Christian community. To claim personal salvation yet deny the need for church is a "contradiction in terms."[14] It is to misunderstand the nature of church and salvation. Salvation is not merely an individual matter; it has implications for community. The church is the family of God. To belong to Christ is to belong to that family, for better or for worse. No one is saved alone. Each of us comes to salvation through the influence, however imperfect or indirect, of persons who themselves belong to the church. We are carried to salvation by persons who arrived before us. In that sense, there is no salvation outside the church.

The church itself does not save anyone; God alone brings salvation. The church does not mechanically dispense salvation to some and deny it to others. As Karl Barth suggested, the church is a secondary "token" of God's salvation. The primary vehicle is found in Christ alone.[15] Even though it is secondary, the church is inseparably related to Christ and His saving work. The church does not save, but it is the vehicle which God has chosen to make known salvation and in which salvation may be nurtured.

We do not use the phrase "no salvation outside the church" to "threaten or damn those outside the church, but to interpret it as a hope and promise for ourselves and our community." We would be better served to say, "Salvation inside the Church"![16]

The Church at Worship

No other occasion unites the church as powerfully and dramatically as does its worship. In worship the Word is preached, taught, and experienced within the community of faith. Worship is the witness of the church to the saving power of the gospel. Worship is the place in which the church affirms and reaffirms the presence of God in the world and in the believing community. The church on mission is the church at worship.

James White said that Christian worship is "the deliberate act of seeking to approach reality at its deepest level by becoming aware of God in and through Jesus Christ and by responding to that awareness."[17]

This suggests that worship:
1. requires a conscious effort of the individual,
2. seeks to move beyond itself,
3. is directed toward God,
4. is Christ centered,
5. evokes a response from the worshiper.

Worship is not something we do for God but a response to what God has done for us. Such an endeavor involves a sense of transcendence, an attempt to move beyond ourselves to a deeper, more profound dimension of spiritual life. Transcendence recognizes that God is holy, "high and lifted up," His "ways [are] past finding out" (Isa. 6:1; Rom. 11:33, KJV). God cannot be manipulated; He can only be encountered. God, not the congregation, is the object of Christian worship.

Because God is holy, worship is a serious affair. It need not be somber or stuffy, but it is serious. The church must never confuse the sentimental, the trivial, or the superficial with genuine worship. Worship, therefore, is not dependent on our individual experience of it. It is not validated by the presence of some immediate spiritual gratification but by a true faith response to God. That is why community is an inseparable element of Christian worship. Although genuine worship may occur in private, the church is that community in which worship is cultivated. The community provides a source of encouragement when faith is difficult and a source of confirmation when faith is clear and certain.

White also observed that meaningful worship does not require the presentation of new spiritual insight on every occasion. It more often involves "a rediscovery of the salvation events which we already know—and constantly forget."[18] To many observers and participants, Christian worship seems unceasingly repetitive. Yet as persons hear and celebrate the old, old story, they appropriate its truths anew.

For that reason the church need not fear or reject ritual in its worship life. Indeed, some ritual is healthy and unavoidable. The repetition of baptism and the Lord's Supper provides significant rituals in which the truths of the gospel are repeated throughout the church's life. True, a ritualized worship may undermine spiritual vitality until participants merely go through the motions of worship, expecting nothing and receiving what they expect. Nonetheless, ritual is a healthy and unavoidable element of worship. It provides a sense of security and strength in the midst of the unanticipated upheavals of life. The church which centers all its worship energy on the immediate and the spontaneous may foster chaos, not divine encounter.

The early church discovered the value of ritual and repetition in worship as it developed what is called the "Christian year." By retelling the story of Jesus at specific occasions—Advent, Christmas, Lent, Holy Week, Easter, Pentecost—within the scope of a year the church created a "calendar" for educating new believers and awakening mature Christians to new insight. How many of us hear the same Christmas and Easter stories differently as we experience life from one year to another? Advent, for example, provides a wonderful opportunity for rediscovering the spiritual significance of Christmas and the distractions of an increasingly secularized holiday. Advent simply means "coming." It is that season of preparation which the church observes on the four weeks prior to Christmas. Each week in Advent has a particular theme—hope, peace, joy, love—which calls the church to reflect on Christ and His coming into the world. In my own congregation, Crescent Hill Baptist Church, Louisville, Kentucky, members prepare an Advent booklet of readings for every day in the Advent season. Families are encouraged to use these readings as a part of their daily worship. Members have come to anticipate the yearly "ritual" of Advent as a time of spiritual renewal and revival. In this way children and adults are encouraged to remember what Christmas is "really about." Evangelical churches would do well to rediscover Advent as a good gift to worship and remembrance.

William Willimon wrote concerning ritual that the church's "claim is not that these stories and rites are original or exciting," but that they are true. "In the church the truth is constantly and habitually held before us," that is ritual at its best.[19] Jesus reminded His disciples to remember Him as "oft" as they created the supper in His name.

The Word: Spoken and Enacted

Year after year, the people of God gather around the Word of God. Martin Luther declared that the church is where the Word is preached and the sacraments (baptism and the Lord's Supper) rightly observed. The Word of God should permeate every facet of the church's worship. It is the presence of the Word which makes Christian worship distinct. Following Pentecost, the early Christians "devoted themselves to the apostles' teaching and fellowship, to the breaking of bread and the prayers" (Acts 2:42). Their practices resembled the basic *leitourgia* (service) of the synagogue with two important exceptions: The church preached Jesus as the Messiah and celebrated baptism and the supper in His name. In those events the Word of God was both spoken and enacted within the community of faith.

What is the Word of God? We have already said that the Word is Jesus Christ. At worship, therefore, the Word is the presence of Christ coming to us, made known by the Holy Spirit in Scripture, preaching, prayer, and symbol. Heiko Obermann insisted that the Protestant Reformation was not the rediscovery of Scripture or preaching but the recovery of the Holy Spirit: Christ present in His Word. In the church the written word of Scripture becomes the "shouted word" of the pulpit and worship.[20] The church at worship is waiting on the Word. Every element of worship should be a potential vehicle of the Word of God. Those who gather for worship should anticipate the presence of God's Word in every aspect of worship, spoken and sung, verbal and nonverbal, in silence as well as sermon.

In Christian worship the Word of God is not only spoken but also is enacted in the symbols of the church. Christian symbols convey the Word of God without words. The church has many symbols which communicate the faith—the cross, the fish (an early symbol), the dove (the Holy Spirit), the open Bible, even the architecture and arrangement of church buildings. But the two most powerful and continuing symbols of Christian faith are baptism and the Lord's Supper. These represent the classic ordinances of the church. While there is great disagreement over the precise meaning of these observances, most of the major Protestant theologians—Luther, Calvin, Wesley—would agree with Augustine's idea that the practices represent "the Word in visible form and action."[21] Word and symbol are inseparably related. These symbolic events have no meaning for the church apart from the Word of God. The words *sacrament, symbol, sign,* or *ordinance* are used throughout the modern church to describe the nature of the enacted Word of God. As we seek to understand the nature of these symbols, some definitions are in order.

Word and Symbol

Symbol.—If we should draw a picture of a cross or perhaps a swastika, we could communicate immediate concepts of good or evil without saying a word. A symbol possesses a meaning and a history beyond itself, even beyond words. Likewise, the symbol somehow participates in the reality it conveys. For the church, the death and sacrifice of Christ is forever linked to the object of His crucifixion, the cross. When we refer to the "cross event" or sing about the "wondrous cross," we unite the object (a cross) with the reality behind it (salvation). When we receive the bread and cup at the Lord's table, we unite those objects with the reality of Christ's death and resurrection.

Human beings are symbol makers. Every society, community, and individual creates symbols which aid in understanding identity. Symbols help us communicate the inner realities of our lives. In the church, symbols point beyond themselves to the inner reality which they represent. Thus, we must never refer to a particular observance, such as baptism or the supper, as *merely* a symbol. When we acknowledge the symbolic nature of an object or event we acknowledge that it has significant power in our lives. Symbols are tangible ways in which we affirm the presence of God in the world, the church, and the individual.

Sacrament.—A sacrament incorporates many of the same qualities as a symbol. In fact, the terms may sometimes be used synonymously. The classic definition of a sacrament is "an outward and visible sign of an inward and spiritual grace." Such a definition might also describe a symbol as I have used it here. The sixteenth-century Protestant Reformers did not hesitate to use the word *sacrament* in referring to the powerful symbols of the church. They understood sacraments as pledges or promises of God's redeeming grace. Martin Luther wrote, "In every promise of God two things are presented to us—the word and the sign." The word was Scripture; the sign was the sacrament or symbol.[22]

What the Reformers rejected was the *sacramentalism* of medieval Roman Catholicism. They believed it divorced the symbol from the Word of God and the faith of the individual. An extreme sacramentalism suggests that the outward acts are valid in and of themselves. This may lead to a view of the church's symbols as magical observances by which individuals receive grace and salvation as a mechanical transaction unrelated to inner transformation, that grace is conveyed by the sacrament itself. In its popular interpretation, therefore, sacramentalism goes too far in suggesting that the outward act works independently of inner faith.

Sign/ordinance.—While sign and symbol are also used synonymously by some theologians, others suggest that a sign is simply a reminder which provides directions or instructions but does not participate in the reality it describes. A sign reminds us of something when we see it. In this sense, the symbolic observances of the church are outward *reminders* (signs) of a deeper reality. As signs, baptism and the supper do not convey grace or participate in the grace which God gives; they remind us that grace has come to us.

The word *ordinance* may also be used to describe a sign. It defines an observance which the church is "ordered" or commanded to observe but which does not go beyond itself. Like a sign, an ordinance is an outward reminder of an inward and spiritual grace. Many groups within the church prefer to refer to baptism and the supper as ordinances to avoid the hint of sacramentalism. An overemphasis on the idea of ordinance, however, may go too far in rejecting the mystery of symbols and reducing them to mere observance.

While differing definitions must be taken seriously, the debate over the meaning of the symbols must not obscure the fact that the church's worship is bound together by the unity of Word and symbol. One recent theologian combined the ideas when he wrote, "The sacraments are first and foremost symbolic acts or activity in signs."[23] The church is indeed where the word is preached and the sacraments/symbols/signs/ordinances are rightly observed.

The Word Declared

The church which gathers around the Word experiences that Word in all elements of worship. Yet in preaching, the church looks and listens most attentively for the Word. Paul wrote that it is by the "foolishness" of the preaching of the cross that God has chosen to awaken sinners (1 Cor. 1:18, KJV). The early Protestants used the phrase "the sacrament of the Word" to suggest that the grace of God comes to us mysteriously in the preaching of the church.

A word about preaching.—The church itself is a preacher. All the people of God are called to preach the gospel. While some exercise that gift as a specific vocation, all the church must preach the gospel. In everything it does the church seeks to proclaim the gospel in one form or another. Preaching is one important means of proclamation.

It is easy to criticize the preaching (and the preachers) of the church. Preaching can be boring and trivial, manipulative and condescending. Sometimes the style of preaching obscures the content of the sermon. Some seem more concerned to talk about the Word than to proclaim it. In every age, however, preaching reaches persons with the gospel. Richard J. Neuhaus wrote of such preaching: "It is an Emmaus-like experience in which the scriptures are opened and you recognize Christ, and in him, with a fresh sense of discovery, you see the truth about yourself and your world."[24] The church is always rediscovering the power of the preaching event. As long as the church endures, it must preach the Word of God. The forms of preaching may vary but the "foolishness" of the preaching of the cross must prevail.

The Word Within the Words.—Christian preaching is the Word declared. The sacrament of the Word means that the Word of God works in and of itself beyond the intention of the preacher or the expectations of the listeners. The Word moves outside the proclaimer to do what God intends it to do, often in spite of the persons in the pulpit or the pew (Isa. 55:11). The task of the church is to preach the Word, not to make the Word work. God alone can do that. Every time the Word is proclaimed something happens whether we realize it immediately or not. The church speaks words which by a miracle of the Holy Spirit become the Word of God. That Word enters the lives of persons to accomplish God's will. Martin Luther wrote: "I have done nothing. The Word has done and achieved everything . . . I have let the word act . . . it is all powerful, it takes hearts prisoner and when they are taken, . . . the work that is done comes from the Word itself."[25] Thus every time the Word is proclaimed, whether public or private, hidden or revealed, response is demanded of all who hear.

The Word Enacted

The Word of God is both spoken and enacted. When the church celebrates baptism and the Lord's Supper, it proclaims the Word of God without words. These events are not "mere symbols" or mechanical observances but vehicles of the Word of God. For Protestants, however, the spoken Word is inseparable from the enacted Word. When baptism and the supper are observed, the sermon should address those events. The spoken Word prepares the way for the enacted Word. These two symbolic events define the nature of the church in its calling to preach the gospel *(kērugma)* and make disciples *(didachē)*.

Baptism.—While most Christian traditions recognize the significance of baptism and practice it in one form or another (the Quakers and the Salvation Army are notable exceptions), there is extensive disagreement as to the meaning and role of baptism in the church. This brief discussion can merely highlight the major issues surrounding those observances as they relate to our understanding of the nature of the church. If possible, we should examine the New Testament teachings about the practices of baptism, less in defense of a particular position than an attempt to determine form and content of this particular practice.

Toward a theology of baptism.—1. Jesus' own baptism, while in some ways distinct from that practiced by the church, also serves as an example for the church. In Matthew's Gospel, Jesus submitted to John's baptism "to fulfil all righteousness"(Matt. 3:15). It marked the beginning of Jesus' public ministry and as a symbolic act went beyond the "baptism . . . for repentance" which John practiced (v. 11). The early church viewed Jesus' baptism in light of His entire life, death, and resurrection. The church does not baptize simply to follow the example of Jesus. His baptism was the first step along the way to the cross. So it is with those who follow Him. Jesus' baptism is more than a command, it is a promise.

2. Baptism is incorporation into Christ. Baptism is identification with

Jesus in His death and resurrection. What has happened to Him has happened to us. His death is our death; His resurrection is ours.[26] Paul wrote, "We were buried therefore with him by baptism into death, so that as Christ was raised from the dead by the glory of the Father, we too might walk in newness of life" (Rom. 6:4). Baptism, therefore, is not merely a command we follow, it is a life we accept for ourselves.

3. Baptism is the "door" of the church. As baptism incorporates persons into Christ, it unites them with His body, the church. "For by one Spirit we were all baptized into one body—Jews or Greeks, slaves or free—and all we made to drink of the one Spirit" (1 Cor. 12:13). To be baptized into Christ is to be baptized into community. Every baptism, therefore, has significance for community. Baptism is not simply an individual matter, nor simply an indication that one is now a member of a particular congregation. It is incorporation into that community which is Christ's—past, present, and future. As the "door" of the church, baptism marks the beginning of the Christian pilgrimage. It is not the end of the church's response to persons, but the beginning. Evangelical churches sometimes imply that once they have brought individuals to faith and baptism their major task is complete. Nothing could be further from the truth. Persons do not rise from the waters of baptism as full grown Christians, but as "babes in Christ" (1 Cor. 3:1) who must be nurtured in the faith. For the church and the individual, baptism is a beginning. New Christians are not alone; they are not on their own, but are brought into a community which is prepared to care for them along the way.

4. Baptism is public profession of faith. In the New Testament, the way to baptism begins with faith in Christ. Such faith is an internal work of grace in the power of the Holy Spirit (Eph. 2:8-9; 3:17). In baptism such internal faith is declared to all the world. Baptism is a visual event in which persons identify with Christ. To be baptized is to confess Christ publicly. That experience occurs throughout the New Testament (Acts 2:38,41; 9:18; Gal. 3:27). For the early Christians, baptism marked a radical break with the past and a new openness toward the future. In the baptismal act, the faith of the individual is united with the faith of the community. It is a public declaration of the believer's faith in Christ and desire to follow Him.

5. Baptism is a gift of the Holy Spirit. The Holy Spirit is inseparable

from the baptismal event. Paul said, "For by one Spirit we are all baptized into one body" (1 Cor. 12:13). The Spirit seals the faith of the
believer with the grace of Jesus Christ. The Spirit gives unity to the body
in all things, including faith and baptism (Eph. 4:4-6). Baptism is "the
rite which the Spirit uses for binding [persons] into the unity of the
Christian fellowship."[27] Early Christians and some later Reformation
Evangelicals (such as the Baptists) practiced the laying on of hands
for the newly baptized as a sign of the coming of the Holy Spirit (Heb.
6:1-3).

The Diversity of Baptism

The baptismal practices of the church reflect tremendous diversity.
Our discussion can only highlight the history and variety of those practices.

*In the New Testament church, baptism was administered to adult be-
lievers shortly after they had experienced faith in Christ.*—The mode or
form of baptism was by immersion or dipping of the body in water. The
"baptismal formula," pledges spoken at the time of baptism, varied even
in the New Testament. Some were apparently baptized in the name of
Jesus (Acts 2:28), while others received baptism in the name of the Trinity, Father, Son, and Holy Spirit (Matt. 28:19-20). There is no direct
evidence that infants or even children were baptized. So called "household" baptisms (Acts 16:15; 1 Cor. 1:16) are sometimes used as proof
for baptism of infants or children but they are at best implied and incon-
clusive. The New Testament norm was the immersion of adult believers
shortly after they had come to faith.

Recent scholars from Catholic and Protestant traditions have increasingly affirmed such practices as the New Testament norm, and many advocate a return to those primitive New Testament practices throughout all
traditions of the church. Others acknowledge the New Testament baptismal ideal but call the church to retain its practice of infant baptism as a
valued tradition by which persons may also be brought to faith.

*The post-New Testament church demonstrated changes in the norma-
tive practice of baptism very quickly.*—The Didache, a Christian handbook written in the early second century, (AD 110-120), reveals the
early observances.

Baptize thus. Having first recited all these things, baptize in the name of the Father . . . Son, and . . . Holy Spirit in running water. But if thou hast not running water, baptize in other water; and, if thou canst not in cold, in warm. But if thou hast neither, pour water thrice [3 times] upon the head in the name of Father, Son and Holy Spirit.[28]

An account written in Rome around AD 200 provides an example of the baptismal observance. It incorporates the following:

The candidate is asked to renounce Satan and all his works;
The presbyter [pastor] anoints candidate with "oil of exorcising";
The candidate enters the water, naked, accompanied by a deacon;
The candidate is asked to confess faith in Father, Son and Holy Ghost, the church and the resurrection, and is baptized after each of "three confessions."
Again anointed with "oil of thanksgiving";
Is clothed in white robes;
The bishop lays hands on the baptized and anoints again with oil.[29]

The practice of infant baptism evolved over a long period of time in the church.—Numerous factors led to the development of infant baptism. First, the sincere desire of Christian parents to raise their children in the faith led some to appeal to baptism as a "rite of initiation" which paralleled the circumcision rites of the Old Testament. Baptism became a "sign of the covenant" given to the believers and "their seed."[30]

Second, baptism was increasingly seen as a "sacramental rite" which mediated salvation directly to the individual. As such, baptism sowed the seed which prepared the infant or child for grace.

Third, a theology of salvation developed, largely due to the influence of the great North African bishop, Augustine, which suggested that baptism was necessary to wash away the curse of original sin. Infants, born into the world under that curse, required immediate baptism lest they die without grace.

Finally, as the church became more closely related to the state, first in the Roman Empire and later in Europe, baptism was associated with the Christian society. To be born into the "Christian" state was to be baptized into the Christian church. Baptism was linked with citizenship and a way of admitting persons to the whole society, not merely the community of faith.

Those who practice infant baptism do not deny the role of faith in salvation; they merely redirect its order in the salvation process. Baptism then becomes a pledge (made by parents and church) of faith which is "confirmed" by the individual later on. Further theological problems arise when those who have received infant baptism do not accept faith for themselves. Anabaptists, Baptists, Pentecostals, and other historic traditions reasserted the significance of baptism as following an experience of grace in those who were capable of repentance and conscious commitment to Christ. These groups frequently confront numerous questions in relation to the baptism of children. Given that all the New Testament examples reflect adult believers, when are children proper candidates for faith and baptism? The baptism of preschoolers and young children poses serious theological questions for those churches which claim to practice New Testament baptism.

Baptism: A Final Word

The questions of infant baptism, baptismal regeneration, and sacramentalism have led some segments of the church to minimize the significance of baptism within the community of faith. Such overreaction is a tragedy. Baptism is a treasure which the church shares with those who believe. It is an event to be celebrated as a powerful link between Christ and His church. The baptismal event is not merely for the recipient, it is a time in which the whole community reaffirms its faith and renews its commitment to its Lord. In every congregation, the baptismal event should be a church event full of celebration and promise for both the individual and the entire community of faith.

The Lord's Supper

As the church gathers at the Lord's table it experiences the Word. As baptism marks the beginning of faith, communion marks the continuation of the journey. At the table, the faith of the community is nurtured and sustained. The supper is the continuing sign of the church's unity with Christ. It contributes to the church's identity in numerous ways.

Toward a theology of the Lord's Supper.—1. The church observes the supper in obedience to Christ's command. "Do this," Jesus said, "in remembrance of me." We remember "as often as [we] eat this bread" (1 Cor. 11:25-26). The Lord's Supper is a symbol introduced by Jesus

Himself for those who followed Him. It is the *Lord's* Supper, not the possession of a particular sect or individual church. The church receives the supper from its Lord. Christ invites, Christ serves, Christ brings the Word of God to His people. Admission to the table involves response to Christ, not a particular doctrine about the supper itself.

2. The supper is a source of communion with Christ and others in the church. The supper is *koinōnia,* "communion." Paul wrote, "The cup of blessing which we bless, is it not a participation [*koinōnia*] in the blood of Christ?" (1 Cor. 10:16). In the supper, the church experiences communion—the intimacy of table fellowship. The same Jesus who ate with "public sinners" continues to do so in the Lord's Supper. Likewise, the intimacy which we share with Christ creates intimacy one with another. Paul continued, "Because there is one bread, we who are many are one body, for we all partake of the one loaf" (v. 17). At the table the church discovers its own deep fellowship and the strength to bear one "another's burdens" (Gal. 6:2). To come to the table is to open oneself to the intimacy and vulnerability of communion with Christ and with other human beings.

3. The Lord's Supper points decisively to the cross. The bread like Christ's body is "given." The cup like Christ's blood is "poured out" (Matt. 26:26-29; Luke 22:14-19). To observe the supper is to "proclaim the Lord's death until he comes" (1 Cor. 11:26). The supper preaches the gospel of the cross. Through it the church not only remembers the cross event but also symbolically participates in it. The supper points to salvation secured in and through the cross. It provides a dramatic opportunity for the church to take up the cross and follow Christ.

4. The supper is a thanksgiving *(eucharistia)* to God for the gifts of His grace confirmed in the resurrection of Christ. The supper does not end with the cross; it points beyond to the resurrection. The New Testament passages which describe the supper begin with "blessing" (Mark 14:22; Matt. 26:26) and the acknowledgment that Jesus gave thanks before He shared the bread and wine with His disciples (Luke 22:19; 1 Cor. 11:24).[31] The somber recollection of the cross is tempered by joy and gratitude for the resurrection. The supper is not merely a memorial to Christ's death but a living reminder of His risen presence with His people in the power of the Holy Spirit.

5. The supper is the promise of the kingdom which is to come. In the

Lukan account, Jesus said "I have earnestly desired to eat this passover with you before I suffer; for I tell you I shall not eat it until it is fulfilled in the kingdom of God. I shall not drink of the fruit of the vine until the kingdom of God comes" (Luke 22:15,18).[32]

The supper is a symbolic anticipation of the kingdom of God. Through the supper, the church symbolically participates in the kingdom and anticipates its coming. The supper is a link between the present age and the age which is to come. The supper anticipates the messianic conquest around which Christ will gather His church (Matt. 22:1-14).

6. The supper is a place of reconciliation. At the Lord's table, sins are confessed, repentance takes place, and restoration is secured. No doubt, the early Christians applied Jesus' words to the communion events. "If you are offering your gift at the altar, and there remember that your brother has something against you, leave your gift before the altar and go; first be reconciled to your brother, and then come and offer your gift" (Matt. 5:23-24). If baptism is an unrepeatable symbol of identification with Christ, the Lord's Supper is the continuing source of union and reconciliation with Him. It is at the table where rededication takes place. There the power of God's continued forgiveness is participated in and proclaimed.

The Supper in Christian History

Although a powerful source of the church's unity, the Lord's Supper has created some of the church's most serious division. Even a brief survey of Christian history reveals diversity and division regarding the practice and meaning of the supper.

For the early church, the Lord's Supper was a significant source of fellowship and identity. The Didache records several common prayers used in communion celebration by the early second-century church.

> First concerning the cup. We thank thee, Our Father, for the holy vine of David, thy son, which thou didst make known to us through Jesus, thy son. Glory be to thee forever. And concerning the broken bread. We thank thee, Our Father, for the life and knowledge which thou didst make known to us through Jesus, thy son. . . . As this bread that is broken was scattered upon the mountains and gathered together, and became one, so let thy church be gathered together from the ends of the earth into thy kingdom.[33]

Justin Martyr, writing in the second century, detailed the liturgy or order of service at communion.

After prayers, the people "salute one another with a kiss."

The "president" [bishop/pastor] receives bread and wine mixed with water.

He offers praise and thanks to God.

The people say "Amen."

Deacons distribute bread and wine.

They carry "a portion" to those who are absent.

"And this food is called among us 'Eucharist' . . ."[34]

Theories about the meaning of the supper and the nature of bread and wine vary in the church during the early Christian centuries. With time, however, questions developed as to the meaning of the supper, particularly regarding the presence of Christ in the communion event. The following views represent a brief survey of views, Catholic and Protestant.

Transubstantiation.—This view of the supper, characteristic of Roman Catholicism, suggests that by the words of institution, "This is my body," "This is my blood," the bread and wine at the altar become the very body and blood of the Lord Jesus. Thus believers literally feed on Christ. The bread and wine continue to retain their physical appearance, but their essence, what they really are, is changed. This view, developed by the medieval theologian Thomas Aquinas and other medieval theologians, represents the church's most sacramental interpretation of the Lord's Supper. Eastern Orthodox churches also accept transubstantiation but believe that the elements of bread and wine are transformed during the prayer invoking the Holy Spirit.

Real presence.—Martin Luther denied the doctrine of transubstantiation while insisting that Christ was truly present both physically and spiritually "alongside" or "with" the bread and wine. Luther interpreted Christ's words, "This is my body," as a literal reference to Christ's presence with the bread and the wine. There was no change in the elements, but Christ Himself was present with them as He promised. The Christian experienced Christ's presence in the supper as in all things, by faith.

Spiritual presence.—John Calvin denied Christ's physical presence in the bread and wine, but insisted that Christ was spiritually present at the table of the Lord. The supper was a "means of grace" in which the believer experienced Christ through the promise of the Word of God and the faith of the individual.

Memorial.—Ulrich Zwingli, the sixteenth-century Reformer of Zurich, proposed that the supper was a memorial which depicted Christ's death and resurrection. Christ's unique presence was not in the bread and wine but in the faith which the believing community shared as it gathered at the table to remember its Lord. The bread and wine represented the body and blood of Christ as a sign of recollection within the church.

Ordinance.—While the view of the supper as ordinance often incorporates aspects of the memorial idea, it may also stand alone. As an ordinance, the supper may simply be an observance which the church is commanded to practice. Thus obedience to Christ's command, not any particular experience of His presence, is the primary reason for the church's observance of the Lord's Supper. By obeying Christ's command, the church testifies to its faithfulness. The supper is less a sign of Christ's presence than the church's witness.

The Lord's Supper is bigger than all the theories about it. It is a mystery of faith in which the people of God experience Christ together. One thing is certain, there are no private tables at the supper of the Lord. The bread is one bread; the cup is one cup. The grace which the supper portrays is not dependent on theories about bread and wine but on the experience of Christ Himself. The Lord's Supper can become a source of spiritual renewal in the life of a Christian congregation. When the supper is celebrated, it should be the central element of worship. Hymns, prayers, and sermon should lead the congregation to the table. Ample time should be given to reflection and preparation. The form of the supper might be varied from time to time in order to stress its diverse applications—memorial, thanksgiving, communion. For example, churches might consider using large loaves of bread, rather than the standard fragments which bear minimal resemblance to anything edible.

As the church gathers around the Word, spoken and enacted, it fulfills its mission in the world to preach the gospel and to make disciples as it gathers around the Word. It also establishes its identity as God's pilgrim people bound to the cross, waiting on the kingdom.

Notes

1. Michael Green, *Evangelism in the Early Church* (Grand Rapids: William B. Eerdmans Publishing Company, 1970), p. 51.

2. Ibid., p. 49.

3. Ibid., p. 48.

4. C. H. Dodd, *The Apostolic Preaching and Its Development* (London: Hodder and Stoughton Ltd., 1944 ed.), pp. 21-24.

5. Green, pp. 61-70.

6. R. Newton Flew, *Jesus and His Church* (New York: Abingdon, 1949), p. 169.

7. James P. Boyce, *A Brief Catechism of Bible Doctrine* (Louisville: A. C. Caperton, 1881), p. 3.

8. Dodd, p. 7.

9. Donald Miller, *The Nature of the Church* (Richmond, Va.: John Knox Press, 1966), p. 69.

10. Oscar J. F. Seitz, *One Body and One Spirit* (Greenwich, Conn.: The Seabury Press, 1960), pp. 113-114.

11. E. Glenn Hinson, *The Integrity of the Church* (Nashville: Broadman Press, 1978), p. 53.

12. Carlyle Marney, *Priests to Each Other* (Valley Forge: Judson Press, 1978), p. 20.

13. Cyprian, *On the Unity of the Catholic Church* 4-6 in J. Stevenson, *A New Eusebius* (London: SPCK, 1970), p. 245.

14. Claude Welch, *The Reality of the Church* (New York: Charles Scribner's Sons, 1958), p. 190.

15. J. Robert Nelson, *The Realm of Redemption* (Greenwich, Conn.: The Seabury Press, 1951), p. 177-178, citing J. Baillie and H. Martin, ed., *Revelation* (London: n.p., 1937), p. 73.

16. Hans Küng, *The Church* (New York: Sheed and Ward, 1967), p. 318.

17. James White, *New Ways of Worship* (Nashville: Abingdon, 1971), p. 40.

18. Ibid., p. 41.

19. William Willimon, *What's Right with the Church?* (New York: Harper and Row, 1985), p. 40.

20. Heiko Obermann, "The Preaching of the Word in the Reformation," *Harvard Theological School Bulletin* (October 1960), pp. 11-12.

21. Nelson, p. 120.

22. Langdon Gilkey, *How the Church Can Minister to the World* (New York: Harper and Row, Publishers, 1964), p. 120.

23. White, p. 150, citing E. Schillebeeckx, *The Eucharist* (New York: Sheed and Ward, 1968) p. 97.

24. Richard J. Neuhaus, *Freedom for Ministry* (San Francisco: Harper and Row, Publishers, 1979), p. 143.

25. Gerhard Eberling, *Luther: An Introduction to his Thought* (Philadelphia: Fortress Press, 1972), pp. 66-67.

26. Anders Nygren, *This Is the Church* (Philadelphia: Muhlenberg Press, 1952), p. 11.

27. T. C. Smith, "The Doctrine of Baptism in the New Testament," *What Is the Church?* Duke McCall, ed. (Nashville: Broadman Press, 1958), p. 77.

28. *Didache, VII, A New Eusebius*, J. Stevenson, ed. (London: SPCK, 1970), p. 126.

29. Hippolytus, *Apostolic Traditions*, 21, 22, in Stevenson, ed., pp. 155-156.

30. George R. Beasley-Murray, *Baptism in the New Testament* (Grand Rapids: William B. Eerdmans Publishing Co, 1962), p. 34.

31. Dale Moody, "The Significance of the Lord's Supper" in McCall, p. 82.

32. Ibid., p. 94.

33. *Didache, VIII*, p. 127.

34. Justin, *Apology* I in Stevenson, ed., pp. 66-67.

5

The Church as Spiritual Fellowship

The church of Jesus Christ is a spiritual fellowship. It is a communion of persons united by the Holy Spirit—that Spirit in which all God's people share. There is no church apart from the Spirit of God. "For where the Spirit of the Lord is, there is the one true church"[1] The presence and power of the Spirit transform the church from a group of isolated individuals into a spiritual fellowship *(koinōnia)* bonded in love and servanthood. The life of the church is life in the Spirit. Thus, Pentecost, that outpouring of the Spirit upon the church, is essential to the church's identity and self-understanding.

The Church and Pentecost

The Coming of the Spirit

Reference to both the Spirit and the church appear in the Scriptures before the experience at Pentecost. The church itself had numerous "beginnings"—in the covenant and in the incarnation, at the calling of the twelve and the Last Supper, at the cross and the resurrection. That community which began before Pentecost found new unity, purpose, and power in the coming of the Holy Spirit.

The activity of the Divine Spirit is likewise evident in the Old and New Testaments. The Spirit *(ruach)* moved "over the face of the waters" in the Genesis account of creation (Gen. 1:2). The Spirit came upon the Hebrew prophets, enabling them to speak the word of the Lord (Num. 11:29). The prophet Joel declared that this same Spirit once given to the prophets would one day descend on "all flesh" (Joel 2:28) and that all who called "upon the name of the Lord shall be delivered" (v. 32).

Jesus Himself suggested that the Spirit, like the wind, "blows where it will," moving mysteriously amid those who believe (John 3:7-8). John's Gospel says that the resurrected Christ "breathed" on His disciples that they might receive the Holy Spirit (John 20:22). Prior to Pentecost, the Spirit moved intermittently among the people of God. At Pentecost, the Spirit came with power.

At Pentecost, the Spirit and the church were united inseparably. At Pentecost, the "Comforter," the "Spirit of truth," which Jesus had promised (John 15:26-27, KJV) was poured out upon His people. In light of Pentecost, therefore, we must ask: What is the nature of the Holy Spirit and the spiritual fellowship which the Spirit creates within the church?

The Spirit of Jesus

The Spirit which the church received at Pentecost was the Spirit of Jesus Christ. The church is not left to itself. The work which Jesus began is continued by His Spirit. The Holy Spirit is not a new god or a third god but the all-pervasive Spirit of the risen Christ, a unique expression of the Divine nature. The Spirit is not a substitute for Jesus but brings a new awareness of Christ's continuing presence. As Claude Welch wrote, "The coming of the Spirit does not add something to or qualify or re-place the Lordship of Christ in the church, but manifests and makes effective that same Lordship uniting to Christ."[2]

The Holy Spirit which came at Pentecost is, indeed, a unique person to be experienced in relationship. The Spirit is no abstract idea or mechanical principle but the very expression of God Himself. The Spirit is no mere reminder of Jesus, but the continuing presence of God in the world. Through the Spirit, those who "have not seen" may encounter the life of the risen Christ (John 20:29). In the richness of the Christian doctrine of the Trinity, the Spirit is God coming to us in direct and decisive ways. The Holy Spirit is the Spirit of God, indivisible yet unique.

Spirit-Church

Pentecost is a dramatic event in the life of the church. At Pentecost the church which began with Jesus of Nazareth was reclaimed and renewed by its risen Lord. At Pentecost, the Spirit and the church were bound inseparably. The very faith by which one enters the church is the specific work of the Spirit[3] (1 Cor. 12:3; Rom. 8:14; John 16:3). The *koinōnia* (fellowship) of the church is *koinōnia* in the Holy Spirit.

Yet the church need not repeat Pentecost to prove that it remains a spiritual fellowship. As the church remembers Pentecost, it acknowledges that the Spirit has already been poured out, that He is already present with God's people. The church, therefore, is called to live in the light of that reality and to continue to grow in the Spirit.

The Empowering of the Church

The Spirit which came at Pentecost transformed a sincere but disoriented band of believers into a dynamic fellowship which "turned the world upside down" (Acts 17:6). The Spirit came with power, emboldening the church to proclaim Christ crucified, beyond the bounds of language, nationality, and race (Acts 2:5-12; 15:6-9). It enlivened the worship of the Christian community (Acts 2:42-47) and increased the church's concern to take the gospel to the world (Acts 9:31). Much can be said about the power of the Holy Spirit in the early church.

The Spirit and Community

The power of the Spirit was experienced by the *community* of faith. The Spirit was bestowed, not on isolated individuals, but on the waiting community. The once fearful and discouraged disciples were given a new and powerful dynamic for mission—together. "They were all together in one place. And they were all filled with the Holy Spirit" (Acts 2:1,4; see 10:44-48). In a parallel passage, John said that the disciples were gathered behind locked doors "for fear of the Jews" when Jesus appeared and breathed on them saying, "Receive the Holy Spirit" (John 20:19-22). Again, the Spirit was experienced collectively.

At Pentecost, and in all the church, the Spirit is the great equalizer. Old divisions and distinctions are overcome. Peter recalled Joel's prophecy that the Spirit would be poured out on "all flesh," and sons and daughters would prophesy, young men would see visions and old men dream dreams. Even "menservants" and "maidservants" would receive the Spirit's power (Acts 2:17-18; Joel 2:28-29).

The Spirit descended on those men and women who gathered in the upper room, including the apostles "together with the women and Mary the mother of Jesus, and with his brothers" (Acts 1:13-14). Truly, the prophecy of Joel had been fulfilled!

R. Newton Flew concluded, "There is no aristocracy of the Spirit."[4] Individuals may receive the gift of the Spirit, but ultimately the power of the Spirit must be shared in the community of the church. Indeed, the Spirit's power unites the church in worship, prayer, and common concern (Acts 2:42-47; 4:31). The baptism of the Spirit is not merely an individual experience; it is a church event.

The modern-day obsession with individualism often undermines the spiritual unity and power of the believing community. The Spirit is not given in isolation. He unites persons in fellowship and mission. Jim Wallis wrote, "The Holy Spirit is the source of community and the Spirit's work is more related to the building of community than to the edification of the isolated individual."[5]

The Spirit and the Gospel

The Spirit empowered the church to take the gospel to the world. At Pentecost, persons of varied cultural and linguistic backgrounds heard in their "own tongues the mighty works of God" (Acts 2:11). The Spirit provided the church with the boldness to proclaim the gospel and the willingness to carry it to the world. The Book of Acts contains a dramatic account of their efforts. They preached with power in the face of persecution, imprisonment, and death. They cared for the sick; they raised money for the poor; they responded to the oppressed and the oppressor, to prisoner and jailer alike. In those activities, the church did not act in its own strength but in the strength of the Spirit. Through the power of the Spirit, the disorganized, diverse band of believers in Jesus became a significant spiritual force in first-century society.

The modern church is often tempted to look for power in financial, political, or social status rather than the life of the Spirit. Those worldly sources of power will ultimately fail, however. The power of the Holy Spirit may not be manipulated or purchased as the early church itself learned (Acts 5:1-11). The church's only power is found in the Spirit of God. The church is ever searching for the will of God under the guidance of the Spirit.

The Spirit and Prejudice

Only by the power of the Spirit can the church's prejudices be broken down and its narrow vision expanded. The Spirit compels the church to enter the world with the gospel, to take the good news to those who seem irreconcilable aliens to the grace of God. By the Spirit, Peter learned that "what God has cleansed, you must not call common" (Acts 10:15). By that same Spirit, Saul, a "Pharisee of the Pharisees," became Paul, apostle to the Gentiles. The Spirit was active in the life of Cornelius before the church caught up with him (vv. 1-8), and all "were amazed, because the gift of the Holy Spirit had been poured out even on the Gentiles" (v. 45).

The power of the Spirit continues to call the church beyond its most treasured prejudices. What surprises does the Spirit have in store for the modern church? How will we respond when we are called to those who seem most foreign to the gospel? Where shall we discover the strength and courage to minister beyond our fears and biases?

The Spirit and Unity

In discussing the unity of the church in the power of the Holy Spirit, perhaps one final clarification is necessary. Unity in the Spirit does not mean uniformity of thought and action. The power of the Spirit does not require Christians to become persons who never disagree, fail, or contradict each other. Throughout the New Testament, there is great diversity, even disagreement, in the church. The Hellenist claim that their widows were "neglected in the daily distribution" led to the election of helpers to oversee such matters (Acts 6:1-6). Paul's differences with John Mark created divisions in the missionary task force (Acts 15:36-41). Paul opposed Peter "to his face" when the latter limited his associations with Gentiles to please the Jews (Gal. 2:11).

All Christians possess the Holy Spirit, but no one knows the "mind" of the Spirit entirely. The church is a living, growing organism filled with persons who reflect diverse stages of faith and maturity. All may possess the one *gift* of the Spirit while discovering the varied *gifts* of the Spirit along the way. The gifts of the Spirit illustrate the church's diversity in life and thought.

The Gifts of the Spirit

The Nature of Spiritual Gifts

We must be careful to distinguish between the *gift* of the Spirit and the *gifts* of the Spirit. The gift *(dōrea)* of the Spirit which the church received at Pentecost is the Spirit itself.[6] Persons continue to receive that gift through faith in Christ. We have seen that the gift of the Spirit is closely related to Christian baptism. That event marks the union of the individual with Christ and his church in the Holy Spirit. Baptism into Christ and baptism in the Spirit are not two unrelated events. Those who have entered into Christ have received His Spirit and are called to "walk" in it (Rom. 8:4).

The gifts *(charismata)* of the Spirit are the evidence of that spiritual pilgrimage which the Spirit initiates. They are the "spiritual endowments bestowed by the Spirit for the ministry of the church"[7] (1 Cor. 1:7; 9:30; 12:4; Rom. 12:6; Eph. 4:11).

The whole church, therefore, is a charismatic community in which the gifts of the Spirit are made manifest. The word *charismatic* is not limited only to those who have only one type of spiritual gift. In a sense, all Christians are charismatic as they experience the diverse gifts *(charismata)* which the Spirit provides. The purpose of the gifts is to enhance the development of Christian community and to fulfill the church's mission in the world.

The gifts which the early Christians exercised were not static or predetermined. They grew out of the community's response to specific needs in the church and the world. The biblical writers did not dictate the gifts of the Spirit; they identified them as they were observed in and experienced by the early church. In every age, the church discovers and rediscovers those gifts which the Spirit bestows for the church's own immediate needs and the fulfillment of its specific mission to humanity. The church is a communion in which the gifts of the Spirit are experienced, nurtured, and acknowledged.

The gifts of the Spirit help define the nature of the church.[8] True spiritual gifts enchance the community, build up the faith, and enable the church to fulfill to its prophetic calling. The gifts of the Spirit not only encourage *koinōnia* (fellowship) but also create it.

The Diversity of Spiritual Gifts

"Now there are varieties of gifts," Paul wrote to the Corinthians, "but the same Spirit" (1 Cor. 12:4). With those words, the apostle delineated nine gifts which were evident in the primitive church. These reflect a wide range of spirit-gifts in the fellowship of the church. They are good models for the continuing activity of the Spirit in the church today. Each gift is exercised within and for the community of faith.

1. *Wisdom* provides counsel in daily living.

2. *Knowledge* imparts insight into Christian practice.

3. *Faith* is trust in God, modeled in the community.

4. *Healing* seeks to bring spiritual and physical well-being.

5. The gift of *miracles* creates a sense of awe, wonder, and mystery within the church.

6. *Prophecy* brings the Word of God to the people of God.

7. The gift of *"distinguishing spirits"* aids the church in delineating good from evil.

8. The gift of *tongues* and

9. The *interpretation* of *tongues* may have meant other languages (Acts 2:4) or ecstatic utterances (1 Cor. 14:2).[9] These latter two gifts are the subject of great controversy in many contemporary churches. Clearly, they were spiritual elements evident in early church life. Some believe that these gifts ended with the apostles; others suggest that tongues are a continuing evidence of the baptism of the Holy Spirit. In biblical context, these two gifts are not magnified above other gifts or required of everyone who experiences the Holy Spirit (1 Cor. 12:8-10).

Also in 1 Corinthians 12, Paul listed certain "offices" in which gifts of the Spirit are manifested. These include "apostles," "prophets," "teachers," "workers of miracles," healers, helpers, "administrators," and "ecstatic" utterers (vv. 27-30). Through such persons, the activities of the Spirit are conveyed to the church.

In 1 Corinthians 12, Paul wrote one of his most profound descriptions of the unity in diversity which characterizes the church of Jesus Christ. The church, he said, is a body with many parts, each of which has a special place, performs a particular function, and shares in the common life (vv. 12-26). The diversity of gifts is not to be feared but to be celebrated.

Imagine the diversity of the primitive congregations: rich and poor, Jew and Gentile, slave and free, male and female, the persecuted and those who were once persecutors. Each received the Spirit, each belonged to the body, but each had a distinct identity. Each member is encouraged to allow the Spirit to work as He chooses, "blow" where He will, for the edification of the whole body. Diversity means that the church may be characterized more by its differences than its similarities. Such differences are themselves the gift of God.[10] Diversity should not create disharmony but should foster unity in the Holy Spirit.

The Meaning of the Spirit

Love *(agapē)* is the end toward which all spiritual diversity and uniformity moves. In one of the most familiar biblical passages, Paul described the greatest and most enduring gift of the church: the gift of love (1 Cor. 13). *Agapē* is the fulfillment of all other gifts. This "more excellent way" (1 Cor. 12:31) is the ultimate verification of all the Spirit's benefits.

The church must distinguish between gifts of the Spirit and the "fruit" of the Spirit (Gal. 5). The gifts of the Spirit reflect a diversity of practices within the church which not all believers experience or demonstrate. The fruit of the Spirit, however, describe those qualities—love, joy, peace, patience, kindness, goodness, gentleness, self-control—which the Spirit seeks to produce in the life of every Christian (vv. 22-24). The fruit of the Spirit are nurtured by the gifts of the Spirit in the life of the individual and the church. As the fruit of the Spirit are cultivated, the work of Christ is manifested through the church. Individuals do not keep these spiritual benefits to themselves but express them within the community of faith "to equip the saints for the work of ministry, for building up the body of Christ" (Eph. 4:12).

The Spirit provides the spiritual resources whereby the community of faith is sustained and empowered for ministry in the world. As the church discovers the Spirit in its midst, it anticipates the activity of the Spirit in the world. The Holy Spirit works within and beyond the church. The church takes the Spirit into the world and goes looking for the activities wherever they may be found, inside and beyond the church.

The Church and the Ministry

Every Christian a Minister

All who receive the Holy Spirit are called to minister in Christ's church. The Spirit is the great equalizer. He calls and empowers all Christ's followers to minister in His name. All Christians are called to be "ambassadors" for Christ (2 Cor. 5:20), colaborers with God in the work of the kingdom (1 Cor. 3:9).

The Priesthood of Believers

All the people of God are called "to be a holy priesthood, to offer spiritual sacrifice acceptable to God through Jesus Christ" (1 Pet. 2:5). That biblical admonition is addressed, not to a select group of church officials, but to the whole community of faith. "The whole people, filled by the Spirit of Christ, becomes a priesthood set apart; all Christians are priests."[11]

The idea of the priesthood of all believers has been particularly significant in the church since the Protestant Reformation of the sixteen century. Protestants, led by Martin Luther, asserted that Christ alone was the mediator between God and humanity. Individuals had direct access to God by faith alone. Reacting against the excesses of medieval Catholicism, the Reformers emphasized the freedom and responsibility of each person to receive the grace of God directly from Christ without mediation from the clergy or the institutional church. Whatever spiritual aid the officers and leaders of the church might provide, they did not govern or mediate the individual's right relationship with God.

Luther himself did not seek to abolish the role of clergy in the church, but to place it in the context of the priesthood of believers. He was careful to distinguish between vocation or calling and office. All Christians are called to a vocation of service, ministry, and the "care of souls." Certain Christians perform specific tasks through various offices as distinguished by the gifts of the Spirit. Every Christian shares the same vocation, expressed in various functions. Thus the Christian cobblers or homemakers represent as worthy and as Christian a calling as the clergy or the civil rulers. Luther wrote: "We are also priests forever, which is far more excellent than being kings, for as priests we are worthy to appear before God to pray for others and to teach one another divine things."[12]

The priesthood of the believer means simply that Christ alone is the sole mediator between God and humanity. Each individual may come directly to Him who stands alone between God and the world (Heb. 8:1). In a real sense, therefore, the whole church baptizes, celebrates the supper, teaches the faith, and preaches the gospel. The priestly ministry of the church is reconciliation, intercession, and ministry.[13] The priesthood was not abolished by the Reformation. It was expanded beyond a clerical elite to the whole people of God. Priesthood is not something we reject or delegate. It is a ministry in which the whole church shares.

The Freedom of the Christian

As a "royal priesthood," Christians are endowed with the freedom of a new relationship with God and with other human beings. Such freedom is never understood in isolation, but in the community of the church. It is not an excuse for sin or unbridled individualism, but the freedom to become "priests to each other."[14] As priests, Christians are not free to live only to themselves apart from fellowship with the church. They are not free to believe anything they wish apart from the nurture and guidance of the spiritual community. Rather, radical Christian freedom means that neither church nor clergy, society nor government may obstruct the direct access of the individual to God.

Radical freedom also involves radical responsibility. This "soul liberty," as most Evangelicals call it, also demands "soul responsibility." Individuals who are free to accept or reject commitment to Christ are responsible for the commitments they do or do not make. The priesthood of the Christian must continually be expressed in relationship to the body of Christ.[15] The church is a community of priests, priests together. To come to Christ is to discover the freedom of responsibility for one another. Martin Luther described this "priestliness" when he wrote: "A Christian is a perfectly free lord of all, subject to none. A Christian is a perfectly dutiful servant of all, subject to all."[16]

To receive the Spirit is to be free—free from the bondage of sin, free from the oppression of the world, free to love our neighbors as ourselves. This freedom is not the gift of the state, the clergy, or even the church. It is the gift of the Holy Spirit. The church is that community in which the gift of the Spirit is experienced and the gifts of the Spirit are shared.

All Christians are called ministers. In the most basic sense, the whole church shares a priestly function through ministry in the world. The priesthood of all believers requires all persons to participate in the "work of the ministry." Through the gifts of the Spirit, that collective calling is expressed in the lives and actions of individuals.

Baptism itself is a great equalizer. Baptism is the ordination of every believer into the priesthood of the church. Early Christians (and later Evangelicals) symbolized this by laying hands on the newly baptized as a sign of the coming of the Holy Spirit. Baptism and the laying on of hands made all Christians part of the teaching office—"evangelizers"—in the church. In fact, some congregations continue to practice the laying on of hands at baptism as recognition of the priesthood of all believers. In a dramatic and moving ceremony at a Romanian Baptist Church in Chicago, Illinois, the newly baptized Christians kneel at the front of the church and receive the laying on of hands from pastors and deacons. All who put on Christ become His ministers!

The Office of Minister

The *vocation* of minister belongs to all Christians. The *office* of minister may be applied to those who fulfill a particular calling and function within the church. The early Christians acted as people of God in their witness to the world but organized their congregations to include certain specific ministerial offices. The leadership evolved with the needs and growth of the churches. Those earliest Christian communities depended on apostolic leadership and the guidance of the Holy Spirit through the exercise of various spiritual gifts. Leaders provided both spiritual edification and pastoral response to the needs of the congregations. The seven persons chosen to assist the apostles (Acts 6:1-6) were selected in response to a particular crisis in the Jerusalem church. Paul and Silas were "set apart" by the laying on of hands for a specific mission by the church. That was not an official ordination to congregational leadership (Acts 13:2-3), however. It was a commissioning for missionary service.

As the church sought to proclaim the gospel and instruct persons in the faith, certain ministerial offices developed. The evolution of those offices is difficult to trace precisely. In the beginning, the leadership of the apostles and the exercise of various spiritual gifts provided guidance for the fledgling congregations. Certain traveling "charismatics" (those who manifested specific spiritual gifts) apparently moved from place to place, bringing spiritual insight and direction to the faithful. Apostles, prophets, teachers, evangelists, and others (1 Cor. 12:28) occupied a significant place of authority in the churches. Gradually the churches also turned for leadership to a more settled, less itinerant group of persons. The New Testament uses such words as presbyter or elder (*presbuteros*), bishop (*episkopos*) and deacon (*diakonos*) to refer to this ministry. In the New Testament, presbyter, elder, and bishop are often used interchangeably to refer to the pastoral office. In its earliest form, this office parallelled that of the elders who presided over the Jewish synagogue.[17] Such persons served as spiritual guides and examples for the churches. The office of deacon or "helper" was given to those particularly charged with caring for the practical needs of the community.

Forms of the Ministry

Christian ministry is expressed in various forms and offices. Roman Catholic, Anglican, and Eastern Orthodox communions have a more elaborate hierarchy of ministers which include archbishops, bishops, priests, deacons, and other ministerial offices. Each stands in a particular line of authority believed to be traced to the apostolic tradition of the church.

The Presbyterian-Reformed churches promote a fourfold ministry composed of pastors, teachers, deacons, and elders (the latter not ordained). Congregational, Baptist, and other Free Churches tend toward a twofold ministerial office found in pastors/elders and deacons. Quakers and other spiritualist groups stress the ministerial calling of all church members. Some churches ordain only celibate males, others ordain only males (married or single), while others ordain both males and females to the ministry. Many ordain only those who fulfill priestly or pastoral functions while some communions ordain for specific ministries—evangelism, music ministry, counseling, religious education, missions, and other areas of service. In some traditions and congregations, the minister is an authority figure who represents Christ in the church and carries particular authority for proclaiming the Word. As "God's anointed," the minister occupies a peculiar place in the divine scheme of things as interpreter of the Word of God. Another understanding of the ministry is found in the role of the minister as professional. Specially trained to perform certain ministerial functions, the minister is a professional who provides particular and necessary functions. It recognizes the diversity of gifts and the inability of every minister to do everything effectively. Perhaps a more inclusive form of ministry is that of the minister as vehicle of the Word of God. As an instrument of God's Word, the minister may at times speak prophetically and authoritatively a "thus saith the Lord" to the church and the world. As vehicle of the Word, the minister may also exercise specific functions as a trained professional. But the center of ministry is not found in authoritarianism or professionalism but in openness to the Word and Spirit of God. Ministry begins with grace and vulnerability—a recognition that the Word of God has come to one human life with a word for all others. Whatever function they may fulfill, whatever title they retain, ministers begin with captivity to the Word of God.

Ministerial Leadership

What do ministerial leaders contribute to the community of faith? They are "overseers" of the people of God, upholding apostolic teaching and providing instruction for the faithful (Acts 20:28-35).

As good shepherds, they are "willingly" and "eagerly" to care for God's "flock," "not as domineering over those in your charge, but being examples." In this regard, they are overseers "of the community," representing Christ who is the "chief Shepherd" of all the church (1 Pet. 5:1-4).

In the most profound sense, the office of minister is related to one who is the "servant of the Word of God." The minister brings God's word to the church as Christ did, "in the form of a servant." Ministry in contemporary churches may take many different forms not evident in the New Testament. The calling, however, remains the same: to bring the Word of God to the people of God.[18]

The calling to the office of ministry begins, as do all callings in the church, as a gift of the Holy Spirit. Again, Scripture seems clear that all Christians are called to ministry. Yet it also indicates that certain persons do receive a call to particular tasks. Frank Stagg observed, "The mystery cannot be completely dispelled. For reasons known only to God, he seems to call some to be 'ministers' in a sense not common to all his people."[19] Indeed, some who are called seem the least likely of candidates (for example, Moses, Deborah, Jeremiah, Elijah, Matthew, Simon Peter and the other ten apostles). The call begins with the Holy Spirit, is imparted to the individual, and is recognized within the community. The recognition of an individual's calling and its meaning for the church involves the question of ministerial authority and ordination.

The Ministry and Authority

No discussion of the nature of the church and its ministry can ignore the question of ministerial authority. With the growth of the church and the death of the apostles, the early Christians turned increasingly to the ministerial office for direction and leadership. That development, to some extent inevitable, resulted in a growing distinction between clergy and laity in the church.

The Rise of the Clergy

Numerous developments influenced the church's understanding of ministerial authority. By the end of the first century, tensions increased between the traveling charismatics and the more settled local pastors. As early as AD 96, Clement, pastor of the church at Rome, addressed such a conflict in the problem-plagued church at Corinth. According to Clement, a group of "prophets" had taken over the troubled Corinthian church, deposing the pastors and deacons, those duly recognized representatives of Christ. Clement urged that the "instigators of the revolt" "submit to their elders" and that the faithful servants be restored.[20]

The Didache, written in the early second century, suggests a procedure for dealing with such prophets who might appear in the church from time to time. The advice is this:

> Every apostle who comes to you should be received as the Lord. But he should not remain more than one day, and if there is some necessity a second as well, but if he should remain three, he is a false prophet . . . he should receive nothing but bread until he finds his next lodging. But if he requests money, he is a false prophet.[21]

Increasingly, therefore, the church grew wary of the traveling charismatics and turned to the settled pastors and deacons as the chief ministerial authority for the community.

By the third and fourth centuries, the church had begun to distinguish between the office of bishop *(episkopos)* and presbyter *(presbuteros)*. Bishops were senior pastors whose wisdom and faith were exemplary. They provided a continuing link to the apostles and, through them, to Christ. So Ignatius of Antioch, writing in the second century, could suggest, "Apart from the bishop no one is to do anything pertaining to the church."[22] By the third and fourth centuries, bishops were recognized as the chief spiritual and administrative officers of the church. Through the bishop's authority, the church performed its ministry. Bishops, presbyters, and deacons thus provided the threefold ministerial leadership of the church, an authority conferred by ordination. These professional ministers were distinguished from the church's nonordained laity *(laikos)*.

Ordination for Ministry

By virtue of ordination, the authority of Christ was passed on to the apostles and to the bishops for the church. The doctrine of apostolic succession means that the authority of the church is extended to every age through the office of bishop. Ordination, while not clearly developed in the New Testament, soon became in important sign of ministerial authority within the church. The New Testament contains four passages which refer to the laying on of hands in a way which may be related to ordination.

In Acts 6:6, hands were laid on the seven persons chosen to help the apostles. In Acts 13:3 Barnabas and Saul received the laying on of hands for a particular missionary task. This seems more a commissioning than a rite of ordination.[23] Two other texts—1 Timothy 4:14 and 2 Timothy 1:6—refer to Timothy's having received the gift of God at the laying on of hands. But this provides no clear-cut evidence that the practice was normative for presbyters in the early church or that Timothy himself was considered a presbyter. In fact, the Greek word *cheirotonein*, which might be translated "ordain," might also be rendered "appoint."[24]

We may conclude, therefore, that ordination as practiced in the modern church, Catholic and Protestant, has no precise parallel in the New

Testament community. At its best, the practice of ordaining ministers provides a means by which the church commissions, encourages, even participates in the call to Christian ministry. At worst, ordination might create an artificial division between clergy and laity, undermining the universal ministry of all Christians. Ordination can be a significant experience for the individual and the community of faith, a time when gifts are affirmed, a call is celebrated, and a minister is "sent out." It is not a practice which the church can or should soon relinquish. Perhaps the contemporary church should distinguish between authoritative and authoritarian ministry in the church. Authoritative ministry brings the Word of the Lord—prophetic, challenging, reconciling, redeeming—to the people. It recognizes a particular call to specific ministry among the entire community of ministers, the church. An authoritarian ministry might foster control, manipulation, and second-class status for the non-ordained. The modern church must continue to struggle against the tendency to "clergify" the church through ordination by creating an official, tax-exempt class of professisonal ministers who assume another status than that of servants of the Word.

The Church and Spirituality

Ministry, whatever form it may take, involves the spiritual nurture of the people of God. As a spiritual fellowship, the church is called to nurture Christian spirituality among its members. Spirituality is that process of continued spiritual growth and renewal in the grace and knowledge of God. Spirituality is the Christian's continuing experience of life in the Spirit.

A Theology of Spirituality

We have already suggested that spiritual instruction is one facet of the church's teaching ministry. At its best, the church instructs persons in the spiritual life while providing a community in which spiritual exploration and experience may be cultivated. The goal of genuine spirituality is a deeper relationship with God and not to become more pious. Through spiritual experience, individuals become more aware of God, not their own spirituality. Spiritual exploration leads us to recognize spiritual vulnerability. Few genuine models of true spirituality would consider themselves "spiritual." They sought to practice the presence of God, not to achieve status as the church's spiritual elite.

Neither is spirituality mere religious respectability. There is no guarantee that the observance of certain religious practices will produce a more intimate relationship with God. It may simply make us more respectable sinners than those whose wrongs are more blatant than our own (Luke 18:9-14). Spirituality is not a Christian self-help program or a means of securing material possessions or social status. It is a desire to know God, whatever circumstance may bring.

Spirituality involves a sense of grace and dependence. The spiritual life begins with God's grace. Only by grace do we experience the Spirit. Dependence or humility is the recognition that there are no self-made men and women. All are debtors to God and other persons for life and breath. Dependence means recognizing the truth about ourselves and casting ourselves on God. The response which we make to divine grace is an act of faith. Faith is not merely accepting a set of propositions about Jesus. Faith as a response to grace means realizing that *Jesus knows me* and that I am continually being accepted by Him. Even when faith is difficult, we cling to Jesus and His faithfulness to us. Such a spirituality encompasses the entire life of the individual. It is manifest in surprise and spontaneity, as well as discipline and order.

The Practice of the Presence

In the community of faith, persons receive both instruction and participation in the life of the Spirit. The church is called to guide the people of God in the practice of the presence of God. The church expresses spirituality in many ways.

The church is a community of prayer.—The church teaches us to pray and prays with us. The prayer of the community is also intercessory prayer. The church prays "without ceasing" (Acts 12:5; 1 Thess. 5:17, KJV), "for one another" (Jas. 5:16; see Eph. 6:18). Such prayer is also based on a deepening relationship with God. We do not pray merely to get what we want, but in order to know God. In the intimacy of prayer, we cry, "Abba! Father!" (Rom. 8:15).

The church is a community which meditates on the Word of God (Ps. 1:1; Acts 2:42).—The church gathers around the Word of God, written and spoken, not only to be instructed but also to be transformed. No one has complete and immediate spiritual insight and wisdom. We are all at various stages of faith. The church provides an environment where the Word of God prevails and where the people of God learn from shared spiritual experience.

The church is also a community of concern. It seeks to turn the inner light of individual spirituality outward on the world. Apart from community, spirituality may succumb to self-centeredness, individualism, and excessive introspection. Spirituality which ignores the needs of the hungry, the broken, and the oppressed is incomplete and inadequate, unworthy of the people of God. The church is a "school of Christ" which unites us with others who are on the spiritual journey and calls us to participate in God's redemptive activity in the world.

Notes

1. J. Robert Nelson, *The Realm of Redemption* (Greenwich, Conn.: Seabury Press, 1951), p. 37.

2. Claude Welch, *The Reality of the Church* (New York: Charles Scribner's Sons, 1958), p. 222.

3. Nelson, p. 38.

4. R. Newton Flew, *Jesus and His Church* (London: Epworth Press, 1949), p. 147.

5. Jim Wallis, *Agenda for a Biblical People* (San Francisco: Harper and Row, Publishers, 1984), p. 80.

6. Dale Moody, "The Nature of the Church," *What Is the Church?* Duke McCall, ed. (Nashville: Broadman Press, 1958), p. 27.

7. Ibid.

8. Wallis, pp. 79-80.

9. I am indebted to my colleague Professor Wayne Ward for this list of *charismata*.

10. Oscar J. F. Seitz, *One Body and One Spirit* (Greenwich, Conn.: The Seabury Press, 1960), p. 96.

11. Hans Küng, *The Church* (New York: Sheed and Ward), p. 371.

12. Martin Luther, "The Freedom of the Christian." *Three Treatises* (Philadelphia: Fortress Press, 1960), p. 290.

13. Küng, pp. 379-380.

14. Carlyle Marney, *Priests to Each Other* (Valley Forge: Judson Press, 1974).

15. Nelson, p. 144.

16. Luther, p. 277.

17. Newton, p. 277.

18. Nelson, pp. 147-149.

19. Frank Stagg, "Understanding the Call to Ministry," *Formation for Ministry* Anne Davis and Wade Rowatt, eds. (Louisville: *Review and Expositor*, 1984), p. 32.

20. *I Clement* 57, *The Apostolic Fathers* Jack Sparks, ed. (Nashville: Thomas Nelson, Inc., 1978), p. 49.

21. *The Didache*, 11.3 in *The Apostolic Fathers*, p. 316.

22. Ignatius of Antioch, *Smyrnaeans* 8.1 in *The Apostolic Fathers*, p. 112.

23. R. Newton Flew, p. 204.

24. E. Glenn Hinson, "Ordination in Christian History," *Review and Expositor* (Fall, 1981), p. 486.

6

The Church as Historical Presence

The Church in History

The church exists in history. It is part of the "ongoing process of life."[1] As we have seen, Christianity is a historic faith. It proclaims that God has revealed Himself *in history,* through the covenant with Israel, the incarnation of Christ, and the gift of the Spirit at Pentecost. As the church lives and acts in history, it participates in God's continuing revelation of Himself.

Through its presence in history, the church seeks to mediate the Word of God to the world. It is called to declare the gospel in every age and to every society. Yet the church itself is a creature of history, conditioned by time and space, limitation and sin. The church is shaped by the very history it seeks to transform. Through the shaping of historical experience, the church is tested, purified, and reformed. In history, the church is always reforming.

Christianity is never practiced in isolation from its past heritage and present circumstances. Within the arena of history, the timeless ideal of the gospel confronts the ever-changing reality of human life. Neither does the church read Holy Scripture apart from the legacy of history. We do not leap from the New Testament era to the present as if nothing had happened in between. Those who unite with Christ's church inherit a history which inevitably influences their understanding of the gospel. Knowingly or unknowingly, we are debtors to those who have gone before us, who struggled with life and faith in other times and events and whose legacy of faith we have received.

The history of the household of faith, like that of any family, is, at best, a mixed blessing. In history we discover that the church is both

100

faithful and unfaithful to its high calling. It is at once moral and immoral, self-sacrificing and self-serving. Sometimes it endures persecution for Christ's sake; sometimes it persecutes persons in Christ's name. Sometimes the church defends the poor and oppressed; sometimes it exploits them. Sometimes it fulfills its calling; sometimes it fails. Truth and falsehood, sin and righteousness exist throughout the church's history. While we are not bound to repeat the mistakes of the past, we must not deny or ignore them. For better or for worse, the history of the church is the history of us all. We, like our forebears, must respond to the challenge which history brings.

The Challenge of History

History confronts Christianity with a constant challenge. How does the church keep faith with the timeless revelation of Jesus Christ while responding to the inevitable changes created by life in the world? How does the church remain true to its origins while maintaining a relevant response to new historical and cultural situations? How far can the church go in applying or adapting the gospel to changing times and circumstances?

Such a challenge was present in the church from the very beginning. The expansion of Christianity after Pentecost brought many converts with diverse cultural, economic, and religious backgrounds into the community of faith. With time, new questions arose as to the nature of Christian thought and practice.

Heresy from within and criticism from without increased the need for a system of basic doctrine. The need for order, instruction, and discipline led to a greater emphasis on organization and structure. Life in the world raised questions about Christian attitudes toward politics, economics, government, and other social issues. Indeed, history created a number of complex issues for the church almost from the beginning.

The Issue of Church Doctrine

First, there was the issue of church doctrine. The early Christians proclaimed the immediacy of the gospel in simple truths, not elaborate doctrines. As time passed, however, new interpretations and questions arose which required further response. Which truths were essential to Christian faith and which were not? Who was Jesus and what was His relationship to God? How much of Jesus was Divine and how much was human? When did He receive His divinity? At birth? At baptism? On the cross? At the resurrection? How could true doctrine be distinguished from false and who would delineate heresy from orthodoxy?

The Issue of Practical Christian Living

Second, there was the issue of the church's practice of the gospel life. How could the spiritual vitality of the early church be extended from age to age? When, where, and how should Christians worship? Who would receive baptism and how would it be administered? Who would provide church leadership and how would such persons be selected? What would be the nature of church discipline and how should it be practiced? What would happen when factions in the church disagreed?

The Issue of the Church's Relationship with the World

Third, the challenge of history also involved the church's relationship with the world. Could the gospel be applied to different cultures and nations without being changed or compromised beyond recognition? What should be the nature of Christian ethics? What would be the church's attitude toward civil government? Should Christians go to war or serve as officers of the state? Should they pay taxes? Which amusements would be considered "worldly" and which not? What about money and possessions? How could the church bear witness in the world without becoming like the world?

The history of the church illustrates that such challenges have received diverse, sometimes contradictory responses within the community of faith. In one age, Christians refused to fight, insisting that the way of Christ is the way of peace. In another, the cry toward the cross was "in this sign conquer," and Christian soldiers marched to war, convinced that heroic death would bring immediate salvation. Some churches baptize only adult believers, some baptize children, others baptize infants, while others do not baptize at all. Some Christians use elaborate creeds to define essential doctrine while others want no creed but the Bible, and others will accept no doctrine which human reason cannot verify. Some doctrines which the church once defended with proof from Scripture— the burning of heretics, human slavery and so on—it now repudiates. All are related to the unending challenge of history and the church's continued appropriation of biblical ideals in light of past and present circumstances. The challenge of history always leads to the role of tradition in understanding the nature of the church. Through tradition the church often seeks to bridge the gap between past history and present situations. Tradition is one way in which the church maintains continuity with its past and authenticity in the present.

The Development of Tradition

All churches have tradition in one form or another. In its most basic sense, tradition is "an opinion, belief or custom handed down from ancestors to posterity."[2] In the early church, it meant those teachings or observances which were "handed over" not "handed down" to the Christian community, the legacy of Christian faith and practice. It was the whole revelation, written and unwritten, given by God through the prophets, apostles, and daily life of the churches.[3] Paul described the observance of the Lord's Supper as "the tradition which I handed on to you" and which "came to me from the Lord himself" (1 Cor. 11:23, NEB). Tradition soon became that rule of faith, doctrine and practice, written and oral, which the church passed on from generation to generation. As the church faced criticism from without and heresy from within, it appealed increasingly to tradition—Scripture, creeds, and other apostolic teaching—as a source of doctrinal stability and uniformity.

In the late second century, Irenaeus of Lyons constructed a basic statement of faith which summarized the church's beliefs about Father, Son, and Spirit, judgment, salvation, and eternal life. He concluded, "The church, having received this preaching and this faith although scattered throughout the whole world, . . . carefully preserves it."[4] Irenaeus's "rule of faith" contains the elements of a creed, a summary of beliefs aimed at clarifying significant doctrines. Those statements were used in instructing new converts, in the baptismal ceremony, and as basic confessions of the church's most important doctrines.

With time, tradition also came to include the rulings of various ecumenical councils (gatherings of church leaders to address specific problems) and other significant church laws and practices. The Christian writers of the first three or four centuries generally viewed tradition as a unified source of the church's doctrine and teaching. Today, some groups, including Roman Catholic and Eastern Orthodox Christians, view tradition as the continuing revelation of the Holy Spirit which, along with Holy Scripture, preserves the church's identity in a changing world. Timothy Ware suggested that for Eastern Orthodox churches tradition means the Bible, the creeds, the decrees of the ecumenical council, and the writings of the Fathers—"the whole system of doctrine, church government, worship and art which Orthodoxy has articulated over the ages."[5] In these Christian communions, tradition is not a lifeless ritual but a living sense of continuity between the past and the present. Tradition, in this sense, is a formal collection of beliefs and practices which inform the church's identity in every age.

Others in the church fear that such a formal tradition undermines the primary authority of Holy Scripture. The sixteenth-century Protestant Reformers attacked medieval Roman Catholicism for exalting the historic traditions of the church above the timeless authority of Scripture. They reasserted the role of Scripture above the traditions of the church. Martin Luther proclaimed the doctrine of *sola scriptura,* Scripture alone, as the ultimate guide for the church's belief and practice. Luther retained creeds and other traditional observances as aids to faith though subordinate to Scripture.

More radical reformers (Anabaptists, Baptists, and Disciples of Christ) moved beyond Luther to insist on "no creed but the Bible," repudiating the use of all traditions which might undermine the absolute authority of Holy Scripture. They attacked the "traditions of men" as a dangerous substitute for vital New Testament faith.

Yet tradition in one form or another is an inescapable element of the nature of the church. All Christian communities need and create traditions which provide a source of continuity with the past and an identity in the present. Churches which reject formal tradition often create informal ones which are equally powerful in determining the nature of the church. Those who doubt the power of tradition need only attempt changes in worship or preaching style, techniques for teaching or evangelizing. The cry, "We never did it like that before," is the cry of tradition, recognized or unrecognized. Sometimes, without even knowing it, the church places such tradition alongside or even above Scripture. Such a practice is evident in the response of the frontier Baptist deacon who declared after a heated debate: "I don't care if it is in the Bible; it isn't Baptist and I won't believe it!"

Today's innovations become tomorrow's traditions. Tradition itself is seldom static but is constantly changing. Tradition is an inescapable element of the church's life which shapes the way the church worships, prays, ministers, and witnesses in the world. There are no "traditionless" churches. Rather, tradition should be recognized as a means of uniting the church with its past. It should not undermine but complement the authority of Scripture. It provides a means of handing over the heritage of the past to the people of God in the present.

Historic Models of the Church

Tradition is only one way in which the church has sought to be faithful to its origins within the shifting sands of history. It has also developed various models for fulfilling its spiritual task within the realm of human affairs. These models reflect significant divisions and debates as to the nature and calling of the church itself. They illustrate continuing tensions over what the church is to be and do in the world. The models presented here are all-inclusive. In fact, elements of each model are reflected throughout the life of the church. They demonstrate the diversity of approaches to the nature of the church evident in almost every era of Christian history.

Prophetic Remnant—Universal Institution

For some, the true church is a prophetic remnant, composed of that spiritual minority who have heard the call of Jesus and left all to follow Him. The cost of discipleship is so rigorous, the gospel way so narrow, that only a few will accept its demands. Thus the church is a sectarian minority which prophetically declares that the world and its institutions stand under the judgment of God.[6] The church's task is to snatch souls from the sinful world and into the elect community of the saints. Salvation involves a personal experience of grace which produces a radical transformation of life. As God is holy, so His people must manifest holiness in the church and in their personal life. True believers must live according to a rigorous ethical standard required by the gospel. Likewise, the church itself must avoid all compromise with the world. It is the "company of the committed" who have forsaken the world and its corruption.

The prophetic spirit often fosters spiritual renewal and vitality within the community of faith. It calls the church to return to the primitive simplicity and dynamic spirituality of its origins. When the church has grown complacent, materialistic, or otherwise worldly, the prophetic spirit calls the church to return to its original mission. Schism or division often occurs when one prophetic segment withdraws from another segment it views as too worldly or too fanatical. Schism or division often occurs when the prophetic minority condemns the established or existing church order for having compromised with the world or when the parent body casts out those it believes to be fanatical and disruptive to the community of faith. In sixteenth-century Zurich, for example, Ulrich Zwingli led the Reformed church in separating from the church of Rome. Yet Zwingli later persecuted those "radicals," the Anabaptists, who rejected the infant baptism which the Reformed church continued to practice. The idea of the church as prophetic remnant is represented in such groups as the Anabaptists, Baptists, Quakers, and Disciples of Christ. These prophetic minorities reassert specific aspects of New Testament faith and rebuke more "established" churches for turning away from dynamic gospel faith. The remnant model stands within the dissenting, sectarian tradition of the church.

The prophetic remnant model may involve certain excesses, however. Commitment may turn to fanaticism, spiritual insight may lead to legalistic arrogance, and prophetic vision may become corrupted by worldly power. The prophetic remnant sometimes degenerates into a fanatical sect which manifests religious zeal, "but not according to knowledge" (Rom. 10:2, KJV). With time, it may also adapt itself to some of the same methods it once deplored and the remnant may become a more universal institution. The challenge of history continues.

Another model for the church is that of a universal institution closely related to society as an established spiritual force in the community. As such, the church develops a vast, unified, and universal organization and structure for implementing the gospel in the lives of all persons. If the church as remnant withdraws from the world, the church as universal institution seeks to influence, perhaps even dominate the world, in the name of Christ. Through the strength and stability of its history, doctrine, and organization, the church attempts to impact individuals and society. The church, thus, becomes a powerful moral, spiritual, and political establishment sometimes directly, sometimes indirectly united with the state. Medieval Catholicism, classical Lutheranism, Colonial Puritanism, and segments of Southern American Protestantism illustrate varying degrees of religious establishment in their particular cultures.

As universal institution, the church's prophetic spirit is tempered by the spirit of order. Through institutional organization, the prophetic zeal is channeled into tangible ministry and creative endeavor aimed at reaching all persons with the gospel. The church organizes to implement the gospel commands. It works to redeem the many, not the few, through patient nurture and instruction in the faith. Its moral demands call for gradual reformation rather than immediate transformation of life.

Yet the church as universal institution may seek to dominate the world instead of redeem it. Efforts at Christianizing the society may also foster compromise with the world. Institutionalism may lead to obsession with program and organization, not spiritual communion. Rudolf Sohm wrote that the church thereby transforms itself from a sacrament into an institution.[7]

In the early fourth century, Christianity ceased to be a persecuted remnant and became the official religion of the Roman Empire. In so doing, it evangelized much of the Roman Empire, bringing its moral energy and organizational genius to bear on a whole society.[8] The persecuted became the conqueror, and Christian values came to influence the culture. The church became a universal institution which would endure even when the empire itself collapsed. Indeed, some see the unity of church and empire as the beginning of a golden age of the church. Others, however, view that relationship as evidence of the fall of the church, its compromise with the world and loss of its prophetic imperative. They point to the corruption of the church as it sought to retain the worldly power by political intrigue and bureaucratic maneuvering.

The truth is, both perspectives are partially correct. By its alignment with the state, the church did accomplish great good. It also experienced significant compromise with the world. Yet the church did not fall with Constantine. At best, the church is always fallen, in that it is always composed of sinners. Prophetic remnants can be as sinful as universal institutions. No one mode is all light or all darkness.

Obviously, both models—prophetic remnant and universal institution—are necessary in the life of the church. One is not inherently more "Christian" than the other. Each reveals an important element of the church's calling. In Christian history, these models frequently occur in cycles. A prophetic remnant produces spiritual renewal which is carried to the masses through an orderly institutionalism which cools spiritual enthusiasm thereby producing a prophetic reaction. Such tensions often bring schism and division to the church as advocates of each model insist that theirs is the best representation of New Testament faith.

Denominational Organization—Ecumenical Cooperation

In more recent times, the denomination has become another model for implementing the church's mission in the world. It combines elements of the earlier categories, the prophetic and the institutional. In a sense the denomination represents a concrete means for channeling prophetic energy into organizational endeavor. Its primary purpose is organizational. The denomination provides a practical means for organizing the church to fulfill a particular calling, whatever that may be. As Sidney Mead said, the denomination is "a voluntary association of like-hearted and like-minded individuals, who are united on the basis of common beliefs for the purpose of accomplishing tangible and defined objectives."[9] In its earliest expression, the denomination was one way in which diverse Christian groups could organize around particular beliefs and actions in pursuit of the gospel without claiming that theirs was the only true church. The various denominations—Baptist, Methodist, Presbyterian, Congregational—reflected one particular mode for interpreting and fulfilling out the gospel of the whole church of Jesus Christ.[10]

In this way, denominations permitted the churches to express differing interpretations of doctrine and practice without denying essential unity in Christ. They allowed for a variety of responses to diverse needs and ministries. The denomination, therefore, represents one segment of the larger church. It places particular emphasis on selected doctrines and activities within the larger context of Christianity.

Denominations thrived in America and other countries where religious liberty prevailed. Religious liberty meant that each group was free to assert its distinct views unhindered by state interference. The right of one group to its practice meant that it extended the same right to others.

Through the denomination, individual congregations of similar belief united to carry out those larger tasks which they could not accomplish alone. Through denominational organization, local churches pooled their funds in order to build schools and hospitals, send missionaries, and fulfill other gospel tasks. With time, however, denominationalism created increased competition, as many groups sought to prove that their beliefs and practices were closest to those of the true New Testament church. Thus Methodists debated Presbyterians and Baptists over election and falling from grace. Baptists debated Methodists and Presbyterians over baptism by immersion. Protestants debated Catholics over everything.[11] Peter Cartwright, the nineteenth-century Methodist preacher, declared that Baptists "made so much ado about baptism (by immersion) that the uninformed would suppose that heaven was an island and there was no way to get there but by diving or swimming."[12]

Such competition accentuated disunity and fragmentation as Christians came to associate the church with only one denominational expression. A denomination is not a church in the strictest sense, however. It is a means for organizing churches in accomplishing certain gospel tasks. A denomination is an organization of persons who share certain doctrinal and practical concerns and who have combined their efforts in common endeavors. As Wallace Alston wrote, "The test of all denominational practice is whether it exhibits or obscures the unity of the church given it by God in Jesus Christ."[13]

Recently, many churches have turned from denominational competition to ecumenical cooperation in affirming the unity of the people of God. Ecumenical cooperation does not mean the sacrifice of particular convictions regarding the nature of Christian faith but involves recognition that all Christians belong to Christ and can learn from each other. It is to participate together in various common concerns and ministries in the world. To be ecumenical does not require a commitment to one great, uniform world church. In fact, E. Glenn Hinson wrote that ecumenical endeavors are probably more "viable in the direction of dialogue, cooperation, and communion than in the direction of union or merger."[14]

Ecumenical cooperation has both biblical and practical implications. First, the church is one in Christ. The great biblical images of people of God, body of Christ, and household of faith are models of the church's essential oneness and unity. Second, denominations and local congregations alike realize that cooperation is necessary in providing effective witness and practical service. Indeed, local ecumenical endeavors in social programs and benevolent activities represent an increasing source of

Christian unity and cooperation. Third, ecumenism in its varied forms, is also a confession of humility. No one congregation or denomination can fulfill all the gospel, reach every one with the good news, or express every facet of Christian discipleship. In humility we must learn from each other and affirm each other in the calling which all God's people have received.

Perhaps modern churches could cultivate a sense of "ecumenical traditionalism" as a model for their witness in the world. Historic traditions provide a place to stand, an identity from which to reach out to other communions in the common challenge of the gospel. Such an effort creates what Martin Marty called the "Public Church," a communion composed of various Christian traditions—Catholic, Protestant, Evangelical—acknowledging differences but uniting in a response to the challenges of modern life.[15]

Invisible Communion—Visible Institution

Another model for understanding the nature of the church involves an idea of the church as invisible communion and visible institution. This concept developed as a means of separating the ideal of the church from the reality of its sometimes sinful behavior in the world. If the church is a divine communion, the very body of Christ, why has its history been so filled with shameful sins and moral compromise? The concept of invisible-visible church has provided one popular response to that question. In this view, there are actually two churches. The invisible church, whose members are known only to God, is made up only of those who truly believe. In the great judgment, they alone shall be redeemed and the ideal of the church as God intended it will be fully realized. Meanwhile, the church in history is a visible institution made up of saints and false believers. In the visible church, wheat and tares, good and evil, exist together. God alone knows who is His own. The church on earth is a mixture of saints and sinners, awaiting the final judgment when the true church of God's people will appear.

On one hand this idea provides a helpful model for understanding the reality of the church's presence in the world. It distinguishes the church as it is from the church as it should and will be. It acknowledges the frailty of the church while holding on to its possibilities as servant of

God's Word. Visible and invisible models reflect the human and divine nature of the church. Roman Catholics have used the idea to explain why some persons whose lives were contrary to the gospel might participate in the visible, earthly church but were not within the true invisible communion of faith. Protestants used the concept to explain why the Roman Catholic Church, while claiming to be the only church, was no church at all. The true church was the spiritual communion known only to God, not an earthly institution with an earthy ruler, the pope.[16] Many contemporary Christians use the concept as a way of affirming their belief in the ideal church while admitting their frustration with the church as they have experienced it—sinful, racist, and materialistic, obsessed with its position in society.

On the other hand, these two distinctions do not describe two churches but one. We cannot accept the ideal of the church without recognizing and participating in its reality as institution composed of sinful human beings. Like its Lord, the church must take on flesh if it is to participate in God's saving activity. The visible church on earth is no less the church because it is sinful or because it is made up of true and false believers. We cannot love the church as *it will be* without loving the church as *it is* and calling it to realize its full potential, "holy and without blemish" (Eph. 5:27). In this life, the church as it is remains the only church we have. Therefore, we must work to keep it true to its calling here and now.

Historic Structures of the Church

Throughout its history, the various models of the church have been expressed in a variety of different organizational structures. They represent tangible forms through which the church has organized itself, chosen its leaders, educated its members and propagated the gospel. All churches develop some structure sooner or later. As Donald Miller observed, "The body of Christ must have some historic form, or it ceases to exist. The eternal treasure of the church must be carried in some sort of earthen vessel."[17]

The historic structures of the church reflect the church's great diversity. In fact, the church has carried out its message through a number of diverse methods and structures. Forms come and go; they are adapted with changing needs and cultural situations. Uniformity of structure seems less essential than openness to the Spirit. The Spirit must work through the structures, whatever form they may take. No one structure guarantees the presence of the Holy Spirit in the church.

The New Testament Church: Primitive Forms

The early church seems less concerned for organizational structure than for life in the Spirit. It was a truly prophetic remnant, bringing the revelation of Christ first to the synagogue and later to pagan society. Questions of order grew naturally from the church's effort to extend the gospel throughout the world. The diverse experiences of the New Testament church contained the seed of various organizational structures which would later develop.

The earliest gatherings of Christians were charismatic communities guided by the Holy Spirit through the exercise of particular spiritual gifts (1 Cor. 12:4-11). Some even maintained a spirit in which members relinquished private property and "shared all things in common" (Acts 2:44-45). Like the synagogue, many Christian communities were organized around the gathered congregation of believers with leadership provided by elders and deacons. The Jerusalem church, however, revealed the significant influence of the apostles, particularly James. Indeed, apostolic authority was an important source of guidance for the New Testament church. Paul's continued effort to establish his apostolic credentials further illustrates the importance of that office. The Jerusalem church, with its apostolic leadership was the mother church of early Christianity.

New Testament references to "the church" in a particular location—Rome, Corinth, Ephesus—refer less to one individual congregation than to several congregations in a given geographical area. By the end of the New Testament period, each congregation would probably have been served by presbyters (pastors) and deacons. Those leaders met in council to decide common issues and needs. Thus the New Testament ends as church structure is only beginning to take shape. Precise conformity to one type of structure does not seem evident in the New Testament. W. O. Carver observed that the New Testament "nowhere has an explicit definition or description of the Church."[18]

Post-Apostolic Christianity: In Search of Order

With the death of the apostles and the expansion of the church, more elaborate organizational structure became necessary. Charismatic itinerants challenged settled pastors and deacons for authority; schism and heresy produced the need for more uniformity of doctrine and order; the destruction of Jerusalem and separation from Judaism required the development of a Christian system of church polity (government) and practice.

First-century Christianity made little or no distinction between the titles *elder, presbyter,* or *bishop* when referring to the basic pastoral office. By the second century, however, the term *bishop* was increasingly used to describe the "senior pastor," "president," or "presiding elder" who exercised special authority among the leaders of the church. The bishop was the chief pastor of the church—made up of one or several helpers of the bishop. The word *presbyter* was then used for the congregations in a given geographical area. Both bishops and presbyters were chosen by the church as spiritual guides for the community of faith. With time, however, bishops were increasingly considered the central spiritual and ecclesiastical authority for the church and a particular structure of episcopal government of the church developed. It is but one of the many structures which the church has instituted throughout its history.

The Successionists: Continuity with the Past

Successionism is that attempt to maintain the spiritual and organizational integrity of the church through an unbroken unity with the past. In this view, the church receives its authority through a succession of leaders, congregations, or doctrines passed directly from Christ. Successionism takes several different forms. Some require a succession of New Testament congregations which have kept New Testament faith and practice alive in every age. So-called Landmarkists among some Evangelical groups reflect that type of successionism. Others suggest that an unbroken line of church leaders (bishops) is the means by which the church retains authority. This doctrine of apostolic succession means that the church's spiritual life and organizational structure is found in a succession of bishops who stand in a direct line from Christ and the apostles.

All bishops receive direct lineage from Christ by virtue of ordination and consecration in the apostolic tradition. The doctrine of apostolic succession characterizes the institutional structure of Roman Catholics, Eastern Orthodox, and Anglican communions (among others) in the church. It represents what is called the episcopal form of church government. In these traditions, the bishops not only administer church affairs but also are the source of that apostolic authority by which the church teaches, preaches, and administers the sacraments. The bishop represents Christ in the community of faith. The office of the bishop ensures the orthodoxy and integrity of the church.

In the face of heresy and persecution, the church turned to its bishops for the stability and security of faith and order. The bishops received the true teaching from Christ and those who gathered around the bishop had the true faith. Ignatius of Antioch in the early second century wrote: "Avoid divisions as the beginnings of evils. All of you follow the bishop as Jesus Christ followed the Father . . . wherever the bishop presides, there let the people be, just as, wherever Christ Jesus is, there is the Catholic [universal] Church."[19] The evolution of the office of bishop occurred along these lines:

1. The terms *bishop, presbyter, elder* used interchangeably for the pastoral office.

2. The term *bishop* used increasingly for the chief pastoral offices. Presbyters assist bishops.

3. The growing recognition of certain locations whose bishops receive particular authority and appreciation. This was true of certain large metropolitan areas, and places which had been especially meaningful in the foundation of the faith—Rome, Alexandria, Jerusalem, Antioch, Constantinople.

4. The gathering of bishops into councils to discuss common problems and controversies.

Episcopal authority in church government takes numerous forms in the church. Within the Orthodox and Anglican traditions, bishops generally maintain a basic equality of authority. In Roman Catholicism, a gradual evolution occurred regarding the office of the bishop of Rome and its authority as derived from Christ through the "chief of apostles," Peter. Advocates of papal authority suggest that Christ's words to Peter in Matthew 16:18 represented the foundation of the church. "Thou art

Peter, and upon this rock I will build my church, and the gates of hell shall not prevail against it" (KJV). Peter and his successors thus possess the "keys of the kingdom" and authority over the church. The pope, therefore, is chief among bishops, the representative of Christ on earth. Roman Catholicism represents the most elaborate system of episcopal government in the church.

Apostolic succession provides an important element of continuity in the church which does contribute to stability and order. At the same time, mere succession of ordination or ecclesiastical authority does not guarantee the presence and authority of the Holy Spirit. As second-century dissenters declared, the church is where the Spirit dwells, not necessarily where the bishops are consecrated.

The Reformers: Unity with the Word

The sixteenth-century Protestant Reformers rejected the doctrine of apostolic succession and the accompanying idea that the presence of a bishop, specifically the pope, was necessary for the church's existence. The true church was founded on faith in Christ, not on a relationship to a particular external authority (bishops). Luther wrote, "The external marks, whereby one can perceive where this church is on earth, are baptism, the Sacrament, and the Gospel; and not Rome, or this place, or that."[20] The church is where the Word of God is preached and the sacraments (baptism and the Lord's Supper) are rightly observed.

This Evangelical view suggests that the church is gathered not around bishop, pope, or king, but around the Word of God. The Word is Christ, present with His people. Ideally, Luther saw the Christian community as the final source of church authority. Many of Luther's writings advocate election of church leaders by congregations. In turmoil of the Reformation era, however, Luther sought stability for the church in the leadership of the Protestant princes, thus linking Lutheran churches with the administrative guidance of the state.

John Calvin, the Reformer of Geneva, suggested that the church is where the Word is preached and the sacraments (ordinances) administered and where discipline is carried out. Discipline was necessary to protect the integrity of the church and the gospel and to turn Christians away from their sins. He also believed that the hierarchy of the Catholic church hindered the evangelical calling of the church.

For Calvin, as the other Reformers, Christ, not the pope, was head of the church. Since Christ is not visibly present in the church, He has established certain structures for organizing His church to fulfill the gospel. Such structures involve four basic offices: pastor, teacher (doctor), deacon, and elder. These offices form a presbytery or leadership body which represents the entire congregation. Pastors proclaimed the Word, administered the sacraments, and guided the congregation. Teachers (doctors) instructed persons, particularly children, in the teachings of Scripture and the doctrines of the church. Deacons carried out two basic functions: the collection of offerings for the poor and the care for the sick. Deacons carried out the church's direct ministry to widows and orphans, the aged and the infirm.[21]

These first three offices were considered part of the official ministry of the church. Elders, though not formally ordained, were charged with a spiritual task. They were lay persons who saw to the administrative and disciplinary life of the church. They provided formal discipline when needed but were "to have oversight of the life of everyone."[22] These offices characterize the structure of Presbyterian and Reformed traditions in the church. It is a structure in which authority is delegated by the congregation through the duly authorized ministers.

The Restorationists: Unity with the New Testament

All reform movements seek to restore elements of the church which seem to have gotten lost through centuries of time and tradition. The Protestant Reformation was an effort to restore the church to a more authentic biblical form.[23] The so-called "Magisterial" Reformers—Luther, Calvin and Zwingli—retained many traditions which had characterized medieval Catholicism. These included the baptism of infants and the union of church and state. Dissenting minorities, such as the sixteenth-century Anabaptists and seventeenth-century Baptists, sought to carry restoration in more radical directions.

The so-called Anabaptists (rebaptizers) historically represented in the Swiss Brethren, the Hutterites, and the Mennonites, suggested that the church had "fallen" in the early fourth century when Christianity became the official religion of the Roman Empire under Emperor Constantine. Through this compromise with the world, the church had lost its

spiritual integrity and its claim to be the true body of Christ. The Anabaptists believed that they had restored the church of the New Testament
by reinstituting such biblical practices as the baptism of adult believers
only, the separation of church and state, and the development of a community of committed disciples. The Catholic Church was entirely false
and corrupt. The Magisterial Reformers did not go far enough in recon-
stituting the New Testament church. The church could not simply be
reformed; the true church could only be restored in proper New Testament form.

The Anabaptists believed that Protestant Reformers had perpetuated
the corruption of the church by retaining the union of church and state.
For the Magisterial Reformers, to be born into a Christian state was to be
baptized into the Christian church. The radicals insisted that the true
church was composed only of believers who gathered on the basis of
common experience of God's grace. The church, therefore, was a "voluntary association" of regenerated human beings.[24] The church was organized not around apostolic succession of bishops but a spiritual lineage
of those who shared a common experience of grace and reconciliation to
God. Christ was the true head of the church and His authority was made
known through the congregation of the redeemed. The congregation
chose its leaders and disciplined its members. The Christian life was a
life of discipleship which required rigorous spiritual and ethical standards. Such a life often produced ridicule and persecution. Suffering,
therefore, was considered an inescapable element of the early Anabaptist
witness.

Though developing from a number of historical movements and influences, seventeenth-century Baptists and nineteenth-century Disciples of
Christ mirror many of the Anabaptist views on the nature of the church.
Baptists grew directly out of English Separatism, an effort of certain
Puritans to restore the true church in separation from the false religion of
the Church of England. Separatists sought to restore the church as a
gathered community bound by a covenant with God and one another.
Like the Anabaptists, the Baptists believed that the church was composed only of regenerate members, grounded in the authority of Scripture and under the authority of Christ expressed in the congregation of
believers. In this they also claimed to have restored the church in its
primitive New Testament simplicity. These churches were governed by

the congregation which delegated leadership authority to two church officers—pastors and deacons.

The Disciples of Christ or Christian churches were restorationists extraordinaire. They claimed to have restored the church which had been lost in the multitude of denominations and other "traditions of men" present in nineteenth-century America. They rejected all denominational, ministerial, and sectarian titles for the simple name "Christian" or "Disciple." They insisted that they maintained the true pattern of salvation by faith, baptism "for the remission of sins," and no creed but the Bible. Their brand of primitivism thrived on the American frontier.

Restorationism clearly reflects the model of the church as prophetic remnant. It usually begins as a minority, sectarian element within the church. It calls the church to be faithful to its biblical origins and seeks to reestablish the biblical model in the present day. At the same time, restorationism may create a false security for the church which believes that it fulfills its calling simply by observing certain New Testament practices and procedures. New Testament observances are no substitutes for the continuing power of the Holy Spirit. The church is known by what it *does,* not by what it *did.* The people of the Spirit are the true church responding as boldly and uniquely to contemporary culture as the ancient Christians responded to theirs, building on valued traditions while discarding those which inhibit the Spirit's activity in the new age.

The Charismatics: Unity with the Spirit

Those who represent a charismatic or spiritualist position in the church insist that all institutional structure is secondary, if not irrelevant, to the immediate experience of the Holy Spirit. No organizational form of the church can substitute for the discovery of the Spirit in each new age.[25] The true church is found in those who have received the same Spirit which empowered the first Christians. Thus the church is known by what it *is,* not by what it *was.*

Obviously, the Reformation and restoration movements reflect a concern for the continuing presence of the Holy Spirit. There are those groups, however—mystics, Quakers, Pentecostals, even certain "rationalists"—which place individual spiritual experience at the center of ecclesiastical life. In this view, the church is found in individual encounter rather than external structure. All outward forms and observances are meaningless apart from the power of the Spirit.

The mystics of the church appear in all traditions of Christian history. They seek an immediate awareness of the divine presence which often transcends doctrinal and historical divisions in the church. The Society of Friends, or Quakers, have long cultivated the mystic way through experience of the "inner light" of Christ within. They turn away from outward forms—baptism, Lord's Supper, ordination—for the inner religion of the heart. Like many spiritualists, modern Pentecostals validate the ancient truths of Scripture through direct contact with God in the present. Through the baptism of the Holy Spirit, Pentecostals believe that they encounter the same presence and power which was poured out at Pentecost.

In each of these expressions, the task of the church is to mediate direct experience of the Spirit to the individual. Forms may vary but the Spirit provides the unity of the church.

The charismatics bring vital, personal religion to the life of the church. They call the church away from excessive emphasis on outward structure to the inner reality of the Spirit. The real unity of the church, charismatics insist, is not found in ecclesiastical uniformity but in common experience of the Holy Spirit, the same Spirit which was poured out at Pentecost. In a sense, charismatic Christianity represents a spiritual restorationism as it suggests that the church can receive the same gifts as powerfully as did the New Testament church. That remains one of its most essential and controversial characteristics. Yet genuine charismatic spirituality may also deteriorate into extreme individualism, destroying the community of the church. Such rabid individualism may make it impossible to distinguish genuine spiritual encounter from subjective emotionalism. It may also foster a sense of spiritual arrogance in those who have had special experiences. Modern charismatics encounter numerous excesses in those who too readily promise divine healing, prosperity, and success. Faith is not just believing that something good is going to happen to you. It is believing in God when nothing good is happening to you and you can only cling to God's unseen but ever-present grace. Like all other groups in the church, charismatic Christians must continually "try the spirits."

There seems to be no end to the forms of the church. No one model or structure contains all the diverse elements of ecclesiastical energy and integrity. There are charismatic Catholics, sectarian Presbyterians, and Eastern Orthodox Christians who believe they have restored the true New Testament church. In a sense, all Christian groups may correctly claim to be "Bible-believing Christians." The differences relate to the way in which such groups use and interpret the Scripture as guide for the life of the church and the individual.

The Church and Culture

Whatever form it may take, no segment of Christ's church can avoid some confrontation with culture—the society, government, economics, and values of the world. The church is to be in the world but not "of the world," Scripture says (John 15:19). Yet that simple admonition provides the church with one of its greatest challenges. In one sense, the church stands as the "light of the world" (Matt. 5:14), offering redemption and reconciliation with God. The church confesses that in the end the world belongs not to "principalities and powers" but to God who created it and who will one day bring forth a "new heaven and a new earth" (Rev. 21:1). The church declares that the world is not what God intended it to be. Its word is, "Behold, the Lamb of God, who takes away the sin of the world!" (John 1:29).

Yet the church itself is bound by a worldliness which it cannot completely escape. Its history is marked by compromise, faithlessness, and bigotry in the world. The church seems unable to address the world without becoming tainted by it.

This struggle with culture has provoked various responses from within the community of faith. In his classic work, *Christ and Culture,* H. Richard Niebuhr detailed five different approaches which the church has made to the world and its culture. They are summarized here.[26]

Separation from Culture

First, some Christians demand that the church separate itself from culture, lest it be corrupted by evil. There is no compromise with sin and no room for worldly disciples in Christ's church. The church is a "peculiar people" who should give no sign of sin in its body. Art, music, drama, literature, and other worldly endeavors must be rejected as detrimental to true spiritual life. Thus many of the early church fathers rejected all military and government service, theaters, circuses, and other amusements. Monastics forsook the world for the monastery and the desert. Puritans, Quakers, and Baptists alike disciplined their members for indulging in alcohol, card playing, dancing, gambling, cigarette smoking, and motion pictures. God's people were not to conform to the world.

Accommodation of Culture

Second, some Christians suggest that the church and the culture are compatible and may complement each other. God's activity may be discovered in the world, and the church should look for Him there. By embracing the world, the church embraces the opportunity for reaching the masses with the gospel. This worthy motive is often obscured, however, by the accommodation of the church to the ways of the world. The world gets into the church, and the gospel is compromised. Often, in the effort to dominate culture, the church sells its birthright. Efforts at Christianizing the Roman Empire, for example, led to extensive accommodation. So much so that later generations would label that effort the "fall of the church."

Transcending Culture

Third, the vast majority of Christians reflect an understanding of culture which provides a synthesis—a balance between separation and accommodation. In its relationship to the world, the church looks to Jesus who transcends culture, standing beyond it, offering grace to live in the world but not of the world. God reveals Himself in the arena of human cultures, but His grace is needed to redeem persons from the sin which is also present in the world. So Thomas Aquinas, the great medieval theologian, looked for truth in the works of various "pagan" writers, Socrates, Plato, and Aristotle. He saw their works as preparing the way for the fuller revelation of Christ. He sought to unite the great ideas of human civilization with the theology of the church. Since Christian revelation was supreme, it would dominate and transcend all other forms of culture, however. This represents an effort to reconcile the church and the culture without denying either.

Dual Roles of Church and Culture

Fourth, some suggest that the church and the culture function in distinct separate realms in the world. They have a dual role to fulfill. This position is evident in Christ's words: "Render therefore unto Caesar the things which are Caesar's; and unto God the things that are God's" (Matt. 22:21, KJV). God and Caesar, church and culture, have distinct functions in human society. Government and other facets of human culture preserve order and provide stability for believer and unbeliever alike. The church operates in another realm, offering salvation and grace, upholding an ideal in the midst of worldly realities. Christians then are to obey the duly recognized authorities (Rom. 13:1-7) and trust God to deliver them when such authorities are evil. Culture and religion each has its place. This position characterizes Martin Luther and Lutheranism. It proved particularly difficult to maintain during the Nazi oppression in World War II.

Transforming Culture

The fifth and final approach to the relationship of the church and the culture is that of transformation. Christ transforms the culture. Salvation comes not only to individuals but to the entire culture as well. The church, therefore, is the leaven which works quietly and patiently to transform civilization according to the will of God. Christianity thus accepts the possibility that humanity, politics, economics, arts, and literature may be influenced, indeed, transformed by the gospel. Thus the church's evangelical calling relates not merely to the salvation of souls but the transformation of all of human life by the power of God. In this view, the church recognizes the sinfulness of the world but seeks to remold it rather than escape, accommodate, or ignore it.

Thus the church continues to confess that it is not of the world. Its real life and true purpose lies elsewhere, with God. That does not mean that the church deserts society in order to preserve its virtue. Rather, it moves into the world willing to risk its life for the redemption of others. The gospel is not a "talent" to be hidden but given away even when there is danger that it may be compromised or lost. Like its Lord, the church makes itself vulnerable to the world so that the world "might be saved through him" (John 3:17). Yet through it all, the people of God look beyond the world to the city "which hath foundations, whose builder and maker is God" (Heb. 11:10, KJV).

Notes

1. Howard Grimes, *The Christian Views History* (Nashville: Abingdon Press, 1969), p. 10.

2. Timothy Ware, *The Orthodox Church* (Baltimore: Penguin Books, 1967), p. 204.

3. "Tradition," *The Concise Oxford Dictionary of the Christian Church*, E. A. Livingstone, ed. (New York: Oxford University Press, 1977), p. 519.

4. Irenaeus, I., *A New Eusebius*, J. Stevenson, ed. (London: SPCK, 1970), p. 115.

5. Ware, p. 204.

6. Jeffrey Burton Russell, *A History of Medieval Christianity, Prophecy and Order* (New York: Thomas Y. Cromwell, 1968), p. 1.

7. Ibid., p. 3.

8. E. Glenn Hinson, *The Evangelization of the Roman Empire* (Macon, Ga.: Mercer University Press, 1981), pp. 9-31.

9. Sidney Mead, *The Lively Experiment* (New York: Harper and Row, Publisher, 1963), p. 104.

10. Winthrop Hudson, "Denominationalism as a Basis for Ecumenicity: A 17th Century Conception," *Denominationalism*, Russell Richey, ed. (Nashville: Abingdon, 1977), pp. 21-22.

11. Mead, pp. 129-132.

12. Peter Cartwright, *The Autobiography of Peter Cartwright* (New York: Phillips and Hunt, 1859), p. 134.

13. Wallace Allston, Jr., *The Church* (Atlanta: John Knox Press, 1984), p. 7.

14. E. Glenn Hinson, *The Integrity of the Church* (Nashville: Broadman Press, 1978), p. 87.

15. Martin E. Marty, *The Public Church* (New York: Crossroad, 1981), pp. 3-22.

16. J. Robert Nelson, *The Realm of Redemption* (Greenwich, Conn.: The Seabury Press, 1951), pp. 161-168.

17. Donald G. Miller, *The Nature and Mission of the Church* (Richmond, Va.: John Knox Press, 1957), p. 81.

18. W. O. Carver, *What Is the Church?* Duke McCall, ed. (Nashville: Broadman Press, 1958), p. 3.

19. Ignatius of Antioch, *Epistle to the Smyrnaens, Documents of the Christian Church*, Henry Bettenson, ed. (New York: Oxford University Press, 1963), pp. 89-90.

20. Robert S. Paul, *The Church in Search of Itself* (Grand Rapids: William Eerdmans, 1972), p. 132.

21. Allston, p. 102.

22. Ibid., p. 101.

23. Paul, p. 85.

24. T. D. Price, "The Anabaptist View of the Church," in McCall, p. 105.

25. Paul, p. 123.

26. H. Richard Niebuhr, *Christ and Culture* (New York: Harper Torchbooks, 1951); and E. Glenn Hinson, *The Integrity of the Church,* pp. 69-81.

7
The Marks of the Church

The forms of the church are always changing. Various models and organizational structures have been used effectively throughout the church's history. Amid the diversity and divisions over forms, however, Christians have searched for those enduring marks which identify and unite the church of Jesus Christ regardless of its historical and organizational circumstances.

In AD 381, a church council at Constantinople confirmed the long-standing belief in "the one, holy, catholic [universal], and apostolic Church." These marks of the church—unity, holiness, universality, and apostolicity—help us to recognize the presence of the true church in whatever form it appears. They are characteristics which the church receives from the Holy Spirit, signs which come from God. While they may be acknowledged by the world, they are acts of faith within the believing community. They are confessions of faith in the church as it is and as it will be. Thus, the marks of the church are received by the church through its relationship with Christ. They enable the people of God to understand their mission and their purpose more clearly.

The unity of the church is not based on an elaborate system of organization or an artificial union of its members but on the "unity of Christ." Church unity is unity derived from participation in Christ's body.[1] The holiness of the church does not rest on the holiness of its members but on the holiness of Christ, its head. The holiness of the church is a result of Christ's redeeming and sanctifying work in behalf of human beings.

The universality of the church is not found in its worldwide presence but in the "limitless authority of Christ."[2] Wherever Christ reigns, there is the church. The apostolic mark of the church is rooted in the mission of Christ Himself. The same Christ who called the earliest apostles continues to send forth apostles with the gospel. The apostolic message remains the foundation of the church's contemporary witness.

Christ is the source of each of the distinctive signs by which the church is known. Through faith in Him, individual believers and local congregations discover unity, holiness, universality, and apostolicity. The church is identified by these characteristics in its past, present, and future. They define what the church was, is, and ever shall be.

While the major Christian traditions—Catholic, Orthodox, and Protestant—generally have affirmed the importance of these four marks in describing the nature of the church, some distinctions must be made. Roman Catholics have generally identified the marks of the church with institutional Catholicism, its organization, doctrine, and hierarchy. While Vatican Council II recognized that genuine Christianity exists among the "separated brethren" of non-Catholic communions, genuine unity still requires some recognition of the primacy of Roman Catholic forms of the church, particularly the authority of the pope. The Protestant Reformers, on the other hand, provided a less institutional and more spiritual interpretation of the marks. They insisted that the idea of one, holy, universal, and apostolic church was meaningful only when rooted in the Word of God and faith. Christ was present in the church where the Word was preached and the sacraments (ordinances) rightly observed. When medieval Roman Catholicism lost its foundation in the Word of God, the Reformers believed it no longer contained the marks of the true church. Thus the Reformers insisted that the true church was a spiritual, invisible, communion of saints known only to God. In that fellowship, the marks of the church were complete. In the earthly (visible) church, the signs were present but incomplete and obscured because of sin. Christians worked within the fallible context of the church on earth in anticipation of the fullness of the kingdom which was to come. One scholar wrote, "Unity, holiness, catholicity [universality], and apostolicity are therefore not only gifts, granted to the church by God's grace, but at the same time tasks which it is vital for the Church to fulfil in a responsible way."[3] The marks of the church are not merely promises which are to come. They are realities by which the church understands its genuine identity in the present. They are blessings to be sought by the people of God.

The Church Is One

The church is one because Christ is one. There is only one body of Christ; therefore, there is only one church of Christ. Paul wrote: "There is one body and one Spirit, just as you were called to the one hope that belongs to your call, one Lord, one faith, one baptism, one God and Father of us all, who is above all and through all and in all" (Eph. 4:4-6). Beyond all its diversity, competition, and fragmentation, the church of Jesus Christ must continually return to that simple confession. The oneness of the church is not an idle speculation. It is a spiritual reality. All who belong to Christ are one with Him. The oneness of the church is an act of faith. It means accepting a fact of the spiritual life.

The unity of the church is grounded in the unity of God and the intimate relationship of the Father and the Son. In John 17, Jesus prayed, "May they all be one; even as thou Father art in me and I in thee" (vv. 20-21). The oneness of the Father and the Son is the same oneness which Christians must experience with God and with each other. It is a oneness built on the intimacy of relationship and trust.

The church's unity is not found in an elaborate organizational union or institutional uniformity among its members but in a spiritual union of all persons who belong to God through Christ. The unity of the church is the unity of God.[4] Christ is not divided; those who are united to Him are united to one another. At the same time, however, unity is not merely an abstract spiritual ideal to which Christians give lip service while maintaining competition and fragmentation with the community of faith. It requires a recognition that we are, indeed, one in Christ and a willingness to act on that reality. Rather than beginning with our differences, we begin with Christ, our "one Lord" who is the source of all unity. Unity in Christ is a mystery which we accept by faith and seek to demonstrate in mutual concern and servanthood.

Unity in the Local Congregation

The oneness of the church begins with the local congregation. There the tangible signs of unity—Word, baptism, Lord's Supper, and mutual concern—are shared. The members of a particular congregation are united, not because they belong to the same institution or attend the same meetings, but because they belong to Christ and have chosen to gather together around His Word. In each Christian communion, the gifts of the Spirit are expressed through acceptance, love, and servanthood. Each member is to be related to the other in such a way that "if one member suffers, all suffer together; if one member is honored, all rejoice together" (1 Cor. 12:26). Baptism is not simply baptism into the church as an abstract idea, but into a tangible flesh-and-blood expression of the church evident in a particular community of believers. Thus it is only on the rarest occasions that private baptisms would be administered apart from a concrete congregation. The specific congregation is a symbol of the family into which we are born. It is a direct expression of our unity with Christ and one another.

The unity of the local church is a demonstration of the unity of the whole people of God. It is middle way between rigid uniformity and unbridled individualism; a unity in which persons willingly sacrifice some of their individual freedom for the freedom of life together. Christians who belong to the same congregation need not, indeed cannot, agree on all things. In fact, genuine unity is not found in regimentation but in a willingness to experience *koinōnia* (fellowship and community) through worship, mission, and common concern.

This sense of unity involves a commitment to the local congregation in times of success and failure, celebration and crisis. One of the major problems with the pluralism and diversity in American Protestantism is a tendency toward schism which undermines the unity of the local congregation. American Christianity often seems a communion of "church-hoppers" who migrate from one congregation to another at the slightest sign of difficulty, disunity, or disagreement. This creates a kind of "ecclesiastical narcissism" evident in those who remain in a congregation only as long as it "feeds me," with limited concern for ministering through the church in good times and bad. They demand immediate gratification for their personal spiritual needs, or they move on. Sometimes schism in a local congregation becomes unavoidable, but surely the oneness of the local community of faith must be sacrificed only as a last resort. Our commitment to the unity of the church involves a willingness to feed and serve others, not merely to be served or fed ourselves.

The Unity of the Whole Church

Local unity extends to the entire church. By faith we are bound together with all those of varied cultures, traditions, and doctrines who confess the lordship of Jesus Christ. The many local congregations around the world share a solidarity of purpose and mission in Christ. This oneness calls us away from competition and a feeling of superiority to a recognition of our common task.

Local churches must learn to share together in mutual aid and encouragement. No one congregation is large enough or spiritually independent enough to "go it alone." Churches need each other in prayer and worship, in ministry and mission. The sense of unity begins on the local level. We need not wait for formal organizations or committees before we reach out to other congregations. We do not need artificial union in order to give witness to our unity in Christ. Significant differences divide Christians, and those differences cannot be ignored. Yet beyond the divisions, there is fundamental oneness in Christ. We can affirm that oneness in tangible ways in our own local communities while honestly differing over specific doctrines and methods.

The Diversity of the Churches

The unity of the church may be enhanced, not threatened, by the diversity of the churches. Through their diversity, the churches reflect the richness and fullness of the gospel. On a given Sunday, think of all the diverse expressions of worship which occur in Christian churches throughout the world! In one congregation the gospel is sung to the sound of a great pipe organ, in another to the beat of tribal drums, in another to the rhythms of a mariachi band, and still another to the unaccompanied sound of human voices. Some worship in elaborate ritual, others in the simplicity of silence, and others in boistrous spontaneity. No one worship style guarantees the presence of God. All who come to worship, whatever the form, experience God the same—by faith.

No one congregation or denomination can incarnate all the varied elements of the Christian gospel all at once. Nor do Christians have to accept only one form of worship, one type of prayer, or one way of ordering church life. In fact, diversity in the church illustrates the "stages of faith" which characterize every Christian's journey. At different times in our lives, we may be helped by different forms of church life, each of which should enable us to experience the "unity of the Spirit in the bond of peace" (Eph. 4:3). I once attended a congregation in New Haven, Connecticut, which had three distinct worship services every Sunday. At 8:00 AM they had a brief service where the Word of God was read and the Lord's Supper celebrated quietly, with simplicity and dignity. At 9:00 AM they had a more informal, boistrous folk service characterized by spontaneity, extensive congregational participation, gospel hymns, and guitars. At 11:00 they conducted a more elaborately organized service with robed choir and clergy, "high church" music, and ordered worship. They recognized that the one people of God respond to many forms in which the gospel is expressed. Whatever the form, they were one people in Christ.

The New Testament church was characterized by profound diversity of approaches to the faith. Such variety did at times create controversy, but it also produced great vitality in the spiritual life of the primitive Christian communities. Hans Küng wrote, "It is not necessary for the diversity and variety to breed dissensions, enmity and strife . . . as long as all have the one God, Lord, Spirit, and faith and not their own private God, Lord, Spirit, and faith, all is in order."[5]

The Church Is Universal

During the early centuries of Christian history, as the church sought to describe its unity more precisely, the Greek word meaning "catholic" or "universal" came to be used. In this sense, *catholic* does not refer to one particular communion, such as the Roman Catholic Church, but to the universality of the entire body of Christ. The church is universal because it extends the work of Christ to the whole human race.[6] As Ignatius of Antioch wrote in the second century, "Wherever Jesus Christ is, there is the whole [catholic] church."[7] The church, therefore, is united by the universal, all-encompassing presence of Jesus Christ.

By the time of the Protestant Reformation, *catholic* had become a word used to describe one particular segment of Christianity identified by the doctrines and practices of the church of Rome. Roman Catholics claimed that only those who conformed to Catholic dogma belonged to the true church. All others were heretics, cut off from the church and salvation. Protestants, therefore, often hesitated to use the term *catholic,* preferring instead to refer to the church as "Reformed" or "Evangelical" or "Christian" in order to describe its unity and universality. In our day, however, we can understand that the terms *catholic* and *Roman Catholic* need not be synonymous. The *catholic* or *universal* nature of the church is a concept and reality in which all Christians may share. It describes the *whole* church of Christ.

Universal Presence

Universality means that the church is present with Christ's people throughout the world. Through its universality, the church expresses the unity of all local congregations and Christian communities which share one Lord, one faith, and one baptism. Universality represents the recognition that each local communion is not an end in itself but a part of the whole church which spreads throughout the earth. In a sense, there are no truly independent local churches. A congregation which claims to be spiritually independent ceases to be the church because it is cut off from the whole. Thus the church local is always a part of the whole church universal. Through the universal presence of the Holy Spirit, the particular congregation shares in the work of all other congregations.

Universality and mission are intricately related. The mission of the church is to extend the presence of Christ throughout the world in order that the gospel may be proclaimed and practiced among all people. The modern missions movement was a concerted effort to carry the gospel to the ends of the earth. Today the strength of the church in what were once mission "outposts"—Africa, South America, Asia—is evidence of the universal impact of the faith. At the same time, universality means that there are no second class or lesser churches; all communions share equally in the same Spirit.

Likewise, the universal quality of Christianity can provide a unity among persons which transcends national, political, and cultural diversity. Who can pray with Christians of other nations and languages without sensing the universality of the church? Who can worship with persons of other areas and tradition without recognizing the common presence of Christ? The universal presence of the church means that the church functions under all types of government and political conditions but remains the one people of God. Throughout history the church has existed under a multitude of political systems and governments. There is always the temptation to identify the church with one particular national program or political ideology. When the Roman Empire was falling apart in the fifth century, many people feared that the church would collapse along with it. In response to those fears, Augustine wrote *The City of God,* in which he asserted the continuing presence of the church whatever the governmental circumstances might be. The universality of the church is a witness to its mission wherever it may be found.

Universal Message

Universality also relates to the church's message. The gospel is not addressed to selected peoples and nations. It is a message for the whole world. Through Jesus Christ the old barriers—ethnic, racial, and sexual—are broken down. "There is neither Jew nor Greek, there is neither slave nor free, there is neither male nor female, for you are all one in Christ Jesus" (Gal. 3:28).

Through its message the church seeks to bring wholeness to all humanity. Wholeness is another aspect of universality. The message of the church carries with it the promise of wholeness for all who believe. As the church proclaims and lives the gospel throughout the world, it declares that no person, however geographically, economically, or spiritually remote, is too far away from divine grace. Its gospel is that all men and women can become new creations in Christ Jesus. The church is universal because its message is universal.

The Church Is Holy

The holiness of the church seems as elusive as its unity. Perhaps the church's greatest failure has been its public image, its inability to live up to the holy calling it represents. In fact, the old rejoinder, "I don't attend church because of all the hypocritical church members," is a popular indictment of the church's lack of holiness. At times it seems such criticisms may be correct. Immorality, corruption, worldliness, and pride continually plague the church and undermine the believability of its holiness. Yet holiness is an inescapable element of the nature of the church. The church's failure to demonstrate holiness does not negate the continued need for it.

What Is Holiness?

To be holy is to be set apart; it is to be absolutely dedicated to God and consecrated to His service. It is to become like Him who has called us "from darkness into light" (Acts 26:18). Holiness involves a moral and spiritual transformation from one way of life to another, from slavery to sin to the freedom of grace.

The idea that the church is holy does not mean that it is completely free from sin and moral impurity, however. Humanity brings fallibility. The church must live with the reality of holiness as it is and the promise of holiness as it will be. Holiness involves the church's own recognition of its sinfulness, its continued need for grace, and its willingness to be reformed into the image of Christ. Holiness does not mean that Christians are better than other persons but that they are different. The motives for their actions have been radically transformed. Thus holiness and humility are inseparable aspects of the nature of the church. The church's holiness is not achieved but received. Holiness is not natural to the church: it is the gift of God. The church is a community of forgiven sinners who have been called to holiness. The church's holiness is not derived from its members or a particular set of religious regulations. Holiness begins with God and is discovered in fellowship with Him.

Holiness and God

The church is holy because God is holy. As one scholar wrote, "It is God who distinguishes the Church, sets it apart, marks it out for his own and makes it holy."[8] As individuals conform to divine holiness, the community of faith becomes holy. Since holiness is found in God, the church can claim to be holy, not because it is at once perfect and sinless, but because it rests in God. Holiness is a present reality because God is present with His people. "As he who called you is holy, be holy yourselves in all your conduct; since it is written, 'You shall be holy, for I am holy'" (1 Pet. 1:15-16).

Yet the church is ever experiencing sanctification—the continued growth in holiness—anticipating that day when it shall be complete in its holiness, "without spot or wrinkle" (Eph. 5:27). Thus the church is both just and sinful at the same time. Such a confession does not excuse the sins and failures of the church but requires the community to recognize its constant need of grace. The goal of the church is holiness—conformity to the image of Christ. Yet on the way to holiness, there is forgiveness and reconciliation with God. As Richard John Neuhaus wrote, "The pursuit of holiness is the pursuit of God."[9] The quest for holiness, however, is not a search for something which does not exist. It is discovering an identity which the church already possesses which it has been promised, and which it has been given the grace to fulfill.

Holiness and Church Discipline

The call to holiness is a call to sanctification, going on in grace. Through the nurture and practice of holiness, the church leads persons toward continued conformity to the image of Christ. This means that the church upholds certain standards of moral and ethical life for the entire community and the individual believer. The ideal of holiness must be expressed in daily living. Thus the church declares the importance of virtue in human life. It unashamedly proclaims the need for personal morality and integrity in the way its members relate to others. While it offers forgiveness and reconciliation for those who have fallen, the church does not hesitate to uphold values, ideals, and standards which reflect holiness of life.

Holiness, therefore, is always related to the question of church discipline. Again, the church faces a dilemma. In its best sense, discipline represents the church's effort to promote holiness among its members and redeem those who have gone astray. At its worst, discipline can degenerate into petty, superficial response to a complex human condition.

Discipline is a negative word in many modern congregations. It is often associated with a pettiness and mean spirit which condemns the obvious and public sins, such as divorce, adultery, or criminal behavior, while ignoring the more subtle sins of racism, gossip, hatred, and prejudice. If it is practiced at all, it is often done badly with little consistency or theological reflection. Yet the church has every right to demand a particular standard of those who claim to follow Christ.

Discipline is not the effort of self-righteous sinners to stand in superficial judgment on others. It is a way of upholding ethical and spiritual ideals while seeking to provide reconciliation for persons in need of forgiveness. Discipline is a way in which the church acknowledges that it is set apart, that its standards of life and ministry have meaning.

Evangelical churches on the American frontier practiced church discipline extensively. Indeed, in many frontier communities, church discipline provided social stability, even law and order. Often it was the only forum in which abused women, slaves, and other minorities could find justice for oppression placed upon them. Excerpts from minutes from nineteenth-century Baptist churches provide illustration.

A charge was brought against Brother Pullum . . . for abusing his Son John and for Swearing.

Brother Baker Ewing is Excluded from this Church for Intoxication, for abusing his wife, and disobeying the call of the Church.[10]

Other actions were taken against lying, stealing, gossip, absence from worship, and a wide variety of moral transgressions. As a central institution in the community, the church maintained extensive social and moral influence through its discipline. As churches became more numerous and membership became larger, discipline became more difficult to maintain consistently.

At its best, discipline begins as a pastoral response to persons who have sinned. It is a way in which the church calls its members beyond the standards of this world to the continued repentance and renewal of the Spirit of God. Sometimes church discipline is administered through the teaching and preaching ministry of the congregation. As the church declares the gospel, it promotes holiness and moral transformation in the lives of those who listen and repent. Sometimes discipline is expressed in the individual relationships of church members who confess their sins one to another and seek a new way of life. In all probability, the public discipline of sinners is a last resort after all other efforts at reconciliation have been exhausted. Even then, the community of faith seeks to maintain balance, if at all possible, between the integrity of the church and the reconciling elements of the gospel.

Discipline is an important dimension of the church's promotion of holiness. It has always been a difficult aspect of church life. Modern Christians must work to develop a theology of discipline which will promote holiness and provide reconciliation within that community of sinners, the church.

Through discipline the church upholds the integrity of the gospel. It proclaims the cost of discipleship. Yet discipline is never a cause for self-righteousness but a means of reconciliation for those who have heard the good news and failed to obey it. Discipline is a means for restoring persons to grace and the freedom of holiness in the church.

The Church Is Apostolic

The church is apostolic in its work and witness. Its unity and universality are closely related to its apostolic faithfulness. The church bears the same apostolic calling as that of the first-century Christians. It depends upon and continues the life and message of the earliest Christian communities.

The Church and the Apostles

Paul wrote that the church itself is "built upon the foundation of the apostles and prophets, Christ himself being the chief cornerstone" (Eph. 2:20). The New Testament term *apostolos* means simply "messenger," or "ambassador," one who is sent out with a particular message and mission. An apostle is one who is a witness to the risen Christ. In the New Testament, the word *apostle* has several applications. First and foremost, it refers to that inner circle of twelve disciples whom Jesus called and instructed (Luke 6:13). The twelve are perhaps the most important link between Jesus and the post-Pentecost church, with a unique position in the community. They had a significant role in the founding of the church.

Yet the twelve were not the only apostles of the New Testament period. Paul suggested that the resurrected Christ appeared to the twelve and then "to all the apostles" (1 Cor. 15:7). He also applied that designation to such lesser-known believers as "Andronicus and Junias," as well as to James, the "Lord's brother" (Rom. 16:7; Gal. 1:19). Paul himself went to great lengths to establish his own credibility as an apostle, a credibility which seems to have been under constant challenge. He wrote to the Galatians as "Paul, an apostle—not from men nor through man, but through Jesus Christ" (Gal. 1:1). He also warned the Corinthians to beware of those who disguised themselves as "apostles of Christ" (2 Cor. 11:13), proclaiming "another Jesus than the one we preached" (v. 4).

Thus the "chief sign of an apostle" was a commission to preach the gospel received from the risen Lord.[11] It is a commission which began with the twelve but was expanded to those who were set apart and sent out as "ambassadors" and "messengers" of the gospel (2 Cor. 5:20). Around this apostolic mission, the church was begun, and it continues to inform the church's identity in history.

The Church's Apostolic Calling

The church itself is an apostle. It manifests an apostolic mission to humanity. This apostolic nature of the church is based less on a direct line of duly ordained successors to the apostles (bishops or clergy) than in a faithfulness to the church's apostolic witness. Apostolic authority is authority exercised by virtue of the church's testimony to Christ rather than the structure of ministerial organization. In its most biblical sense, apostolic succession is "the succession of the apostles' gospel and the succession of the Holy Spirit who dwelt in the life of the apostolic church."[12] As the church proclaims and remains faithful to the gospel it received from the apostles, it becomes apostolic. The source of such historic continuity is the Holy Spirit. The Spirit provides the continuing witness to the risen Christ. Thus the authority for witness is not found in the early apostles themselves but in their faithful witness to Christ as mediated by the Holy Spirit.[13] The apostolic message, not the particular messengers, defines the apostolic nature of the church. Through its faithfulness in proclamation, teaching, and witness to the gospel of Jesus and the apostles, the church establishes its apostolic identity. Thus the church has an apostolic past, present, and future. Each new generation of Christians must choose its apostolic calling anew. It must be overtaken by the same Spirit of the risen Christ who appeared to the twelve, the other apostles and even the church's persecutor, Saul of Tarsus (1 Cor. 15:4-8).

As the church preaches the gospel and baptizes, as it teaches and celebrates the Lord's Supper, it fulfills its apostolic task. It remains apostolic as long as it continues the apostolic ministry which Christ began through the earliest Christian witnesses.

Jürgen Moltmann suggested that the apostolic calling of the church is not merely a faithfulness to dogma but a commitment to apostolic life. The truly apostolic church, therefore, may be called to suffer for Christ's sake, in His name. Moltmann wrote, "Participation in the apostolic mission of Christ therefore leads inescapably into tribulation, contradiction and suffering."[14]

Apostolic witness led to persecution for the apostle Paul and a succession of martyrs throughout Christian history. Persecution is the experience of many contemporary apostles who have declared their faith in hostile environment. Those who claim the power of the resurrected Christ are never far away from the "fellowship of his sufferings" (Phil. 3:10, KJV). "The church under the cross" reflects the true apostolicity of the people of God. Like its Lord and His earliest apostles, the church is willing to lay down its life for the sake of the gospel.

The apostolic nature of the church also points to the unity of the church in all times and to the church's debt to history. The gospel has been passed on to us by a succession of apostolic souls who have remained faithful in the face of famine, peril, and sword. Their witness inspires us to continue the apostolic tradition so that another generation may hear and believe the Word of God. Like those of earlier generations, we are a link to the risen Christ and the good news of God's grace.

These four marks of the church—oneness, universality, holiness, and apostolicity—identify the church from age to age. They are not the creation of external organization or authorities but the marks of the Holy Spirit. They are gifts of grace which the church struggles to identify and appropriate into its life. They are not static doctrines but dynamic experiences which are rediscovered by individuals within the life of the community of faith. Each is a pledge of what the church already is and a promise of what it will become. Thus the marks of the church may be said to have eschatological significance. That is, they are closely related to the doctrine of last things, the final end of the age and, most of all, the establishment of the kingdom of God.

Notes

1. Jürgen Moltmann, *The Church in the Power of the Holy Spirit* (New York: Harper and Row, 1977), p. 338.
2. Ibid.
3. Hans Küng, *The Church* (New York: Sheed and Ward, 1967), p. 268.
4. Ibid., p. 273.

5. Ibid., p. 275.

6. J. Robert Nelson, *The Realm of Redemption* (Greenwich, Conn.: The Seabury Press, 1951), p. 206.

7. Ignatius of Antioch, *Smyrnaeans* 8.1 in *The Apostolic Fathers* (Nashville: Thomas Nelson Publishers, 1978), p. 113.

8. Küng, p. 235.

9. Richard John Neuhaus, *Freedom for Ministry* (New York: Harper and Row Publishers, 1979), p. 193.

10. William W. Sweet, *Religion on the American Frontier: The Baptists* (New York: Henry Holt and Co., 1931), pp. 307, 304.

11. R. Newton Flew, *Jesus and His Church* (New York: Abingdon, 1938), p. 191.

12. Donald G. Miller, *The Nature and Mission of the Church* (Richmond: John Knox Press, 1966), p. 87.

13. Nelson, p. 15.

14. Moltmann, p. 361.

8

The Church as Eschatological Promise

The gospel of Jesus Christ is the gospel of the kingdom of God. From the beginning of His ministry, Jesus declared the good news of the kingdom, saying, "The time is fulfilled, the kingdom of God is at hand; repent and believe the gospel" (Mark 1:15). Jesus also taught His disciples to pray: "Thy kingdom come, Thy will be done, On earth as it is in heaven" (Matt. 6:10). What is the nature of the kingdom of God, and what is its relationship to the church?

The Church and the Kingdom

In its most basic sense, the kingdom of God is "the redemptive will of God in action."[1] The Greek word, *basileia,* which is often translated "kingdom" might better be rendered "rule" or "reign." This reign of God is at once present and future. It may mean the immediate rule of God in the present moment or the ultimate, final, and absolute rule of God in some end time. In the New Testament, the preaching of the kingdom involved immediate preparation for the culmination of all things. Both Jesus and John the Baptizer admonished their hearers to repent and prepare themselves for that which was to come. The preaching of the kingdom, therefore, is to awaken citizens of the kingdom, who will also declare the promise of its ultimate eschatological fulfillment in the end times.

The kingdom of God is the gift of God. It is the result of His sovereign activity. The people of God watch and wait for the kingdom, praying that it will come but knowing that they cannot make it happen. "Fear not, little flock, for it is your Father's good pleasure to give you the kingdom" (Luke 12:32). The kingdom of God comes only from God Himself. Christians may participate in the kingdom but God alone is the author of the kingdom.

The kingdom of God involves healing, reconciliation, and wholeness for the outcast and the broken. Jesus' own calling was directed to the poor, the captives, the blind, and the oppressed (Luke 4:18-19). The sign of His messiahship was His response to the forgotten people of the world. Their healing and reconciliation was a promise of wholeness for all who would believe. It was the promise that in the kingdom all would be set right.

Likewise, citizenship in the kingdom requires a "radical decision for God." It involves a willingness to accept the rule of God in the life of the individual and thus the need for repentance. It is a call to forsake everything for the life of the gospel.[2]

Finally, the kingdom of God demands a kingdom life. In the Sermon on the Mount, Jesus sketched the essentials of citizenship in the kingdom. It is a life of commitment to and confidence in God. It creates people who live by different values and standards than those of the world. "But seek ye first the kingdom of God, and his righteousness; and all these things shall be added unto you" (Matt. 6:33, KJV).

Clearly, Jesus came preaching the kingdom of God. It was the central theme of His message. In fact, the first three Gospels (Synoptics) use the phrase "kingdom of God" almost one hundred times. The mission of Jesus was inseparably related to the proclamation of the kingdom. How, therefore, does the concept of the kingdom relate to the doctrine of the church? That question has divided scholars to this day.

At one end of the divison are those who suggest that Jesus' primary intention was to preach the gospel of the kingdom, not to establish a church. The church itself was a later creation of Jesus' followers when the promised kingdom did not appear. Alfred Loisy, the Catholic modernist, said, "Jesus proclaimed the Kingdom of God, and what came was the church." When the immediacy of the kingdom failed to occur, Jesus' teachings were kept alive and ultimately institutionalized in that earthly institution, the church.

At the other end of the divison is the idea that the church and the kingdom are completely identical. The institutional church was founded by Jesus as the extension of the kingdom of God. Thus membership in the church was the same as citizenship in the kingdom. To be cut off from the church was to be outside the kingdom. This view, particularly characteristic of pre-Vatican II Roman Catholicism, involved a doctrine of the "power of the keys." The church, by virtue of Christ's command (Matt. 16:19), possessed the "keys of the kingdom" with the power to "bind and loose" in heaven and on earth.[3] Dissent against the institutional church constituted a direct challenge to the kingdom of God. Therefore, excommunication, even persecution, of heretics and other nonconformists was necessary to preserve the faith and protect both the church and the kingdom.

Between these two extremes lie a variety of interpretations of the relationship between the church and the kingdom of God. Albert Schweitzer, the great scholar and missionary-doctor, advocated a "consistent eschatology," by which Jesus Himself predicted and anticipated that the kingdom would occur immediately through God's radical intervention. Jesus saw Himself as the herald of that soon to be established rule of God. For Schweitzer, Jesus' concept of the kingdom was closely related to radical Jewish ideas of the immediate end of the age (Matt. 16:28). When that radical event did not occur, Jesus was compelled to suffer and die, offering Himself as a means of hastening the kingdom. When the kingdom did not come, it was replaced with the idea of the church. Church and kingdom, therefore, are radically separate ideals.[4] The disciples were selected to aid in bringing in the kingdom, not to organize a church.

Another view of the church and the kingdom is found in the "realized eschatology" of C. H. Dodd. For Dodd, the incarnation of Jesus Christ is a sign that the kingdom is already immediately present, not merely anticipated. The simple proclamation that the kingdom is at hand means that it had come into being with Jesus. The church, therefore, is already experiencing the life of the kingdom though in a limited, conditional way. The kingdom is a promise which is to come but it is also a powerful reality which the church has already experienced. Thus the early church could proclaim that "the Age to Come has begun."[5] The new age had been ushered in by the death and resurrection of Christ, and the church was witness to that new age in its living and preaching of the gospel. The church must continually live in light of the present reality of the kingdom. Dodd insisted that while the completeness of the kingdom remained to be fulfilled, the fullness of the kingdom was already present through Christ in the church.[6]

Ernst Troeltsch, the German theologian and sociologist, emphasized the "individualized eschatology" of the kingdom. In this view, Jesus' primary concern was to set forth the ethical demands of the kingdom as necessary for every individual. Jesus' message was aimed at awakening individuals, not in founding an organization. The church was a natural, though unintentional, outgrowth of Jesus' preaching of the kingdom of God.[7] For these and other scholars, the question was whether Jesus meant to found a church or simply to announce the kingdom of God.

In seeking to reconcile these diverse ideas, R. Newton Flew insisted that, while Jesus laid down no concrete structure or communal organization, He did create "a new religious community with a new way of life, a fresh and startling message."[8] He did gather a specific group of persons through whom He extended His own message and ministry. The kingdom of God was preached to a particular community which gathered around Jesus. That community was instructed to anticipate, indeed, to pray for the kingdom. "Thy kingdom come . . . on earth as it is in heaven."

Flew refused to identify the church with the kingdom of God, however. Nor did he view the church as a substitute for the kingdom of God within human history. The church, Flew believed, is gathered by God as an instrument for God's saving work in the world.[9] The church is the vehicle which proclaims the good news of the kingdom.

So E. F. Scott declared that the church developed directly from Jesus' message of the kingdom. When the first believers formed a church, they were less conscious of their "creating something new" than continuing the life and message they had experienced with Jesus. "The church was thus the outcome of Jesus' message," Scott wrote. It was called to continue Jesus' work in declaring the immediacy of the kingdom.[10] In a sense, each of these theories of the kingdom develops one facet of the kingdom's complex nature. The kingdom is not yet. It is "a glorious hope," a promise toward which the people of God move and which they seek to bring to others.[11]

In an effort to reconcile the relationship between the church and the kingdom, some scholars have distinguished between the kingdom of Christ and the kingdom of God. Citing 1 Corinthians 15:22-28, Karl Barth and others suggest that the church exists in the present within the kingdom of Christ, anticipating that time when all things will be brought into subjection to Him and the kingdom of God will appear. "Then comes the end, when he delivers the kingdom to God the Father after destroying every rule and every authority and power" (1 Cor. 15:24). The church, therefore, exists within the kingdom of Christ in anticipation of the defeat of death, the "last enemy" (v. 26) and the coming of the kingdom of God.[12]

The kingdom of God and the church are not the same, but neither are they completely separate. As Claude Welch observed, the "Kingdom is present in the church, but the church is not the kingdom."[13] The church, though limited by its humanity and fallibility in the world, represents an ideal. It points beyond itself to the kingdom of God. The church is a promise of the fullness of the kingdom which is to come, but it is also a participant in the life of the kingdom here and now. Through its redemptive activity, however limited, the church provides a witness to the nature of the kingdom. It is an eschatological promise of what is to come. In a sense, the church calls persons beyond itself to Christ and the kingdom.

First, the church anticipates the life of the kingdom in its own life of Christian discipleship. As Christians live the kingdom life—as they learn to turn the other cheek and go the extra mile, to share one another's burdens and bear the cross in a cynical and hostile world—they declare the promise of the kingdom. The life of the kingdom involves a particular ethical response to life. The citizens of the kingdom have a new way of looking at life and relating to one another. Indeed, those who fail to respond to the ethical demands of the gospel may not be citizens of the kingdom after all (Matt. 25:31-46).

Perhaps there is no greater symbol of the relationship of the church and the kingdom than that of the Lord's Supper. In it the church in present time looks back to its past and forward to its future. The supper is at once a memorial and a promise. Jesus urged His followers to "do this in remembrance" and in so doing to declare the death of the Lord "till he comes." Indeed, He promised that He would "not drink again of this fruit of the vine until that day when I drink it new with you in my Father's kingdom" (Matt. 26:29). The supper is a pledge of the coming of the kingdom of God.

Second, as the church responds to the captives, the victims, the oppressed, and the outcasts of society, it promotes that wholeness which is at the heart of the kingdom of God. In so doing it will not bring in the kingdom—only God can do that—but it will demonstrate what the kingdom can and will be for all who follow Christ.

Third, the church must never cease to anticipate the "Day of the Lord," that imminent and future time when the kingdom will come in its fullness and power. In that day the church will cease to be and the kingdom will prevail. The church itself will be united with the kingdom.

Thus the church lives between "already and not yet," between the present reality and the ultimate completeness of the kingdom of God.[14] The church, therefore, is the forerunner of the day of the Lord. The church is not an end in itself, but a doorway to the kingdom of God. Through its witness the church points to both the presence and promise of the kingdom. Through its self-sacrifice and service the church declares that the kingdom is possible.

The Church and Eschatology

As an eschatological community, the church is called to watch and wait for the kingdom (Matt. 24:42; 25:13). That continued expectation inevitably leads to other questions regarding the nature of the Day of the Lord and its fulfillment in the world. Thus the hope of the kingdom is but one facet of the broader doctrine of eschatology. Eschatology, *eschata,* "last things," and *logos* "science," is literally the "science of last things."[15] It is the study of those ideas and events which relate to the "end of the age," death and judgment, the kingdom of God, and the return of Jesus Christ. It is the quest for ultimate meaning in the "end times."

The early church naturally equated the fullness of the kingdom with the triumphant and imminent *Parousia,* or return of Christ. Although they could not know the "times and the seasons," Christians were advised to keep themselves prepared since "the day of the Lord will come like a thief in the night" (1 Thess. 5:1-2). With that in mind, many have sought to discern the signs of the times which provided some indication of the impending end of one age and the beginning of another. Those efforts have led to diverse and extensive speculations and theories as to details of the return of Christ and the nature of the kingdom. Such theories are discussed here only briefly and with particular concern for their ideas regarding the nature of the church and its role in the second coming of Christ. A few simple definitions of terms seems helpful to this complex subject.

1. *eschatology*—the study of "last things" relating to the end of the age, the fullness of the kingdom and the return of Christ.
2. *Parousia*—the second coming or return of Jesus Christ.
3. *apocalyptic*—the revelation or unveiling of particular events—the symbolic language of the "last times."
4. *millennial*—having to do with the millennium, or thousand-year reign of Christ, mentioned briefly in Scripture but having immense significance in certain eschatological theories.

Millennial Theories

Apocalyptic speculation as to the events of the end time has been a part of the church since its beginning. Indeed, the book we call "The Revelation of St. John" (KJV) is best referred to as "the Apocalypse of St. John," that most famous piece of biblical literature regarding the coming of the kingdom. Its references to the millennium—"They came to life, and reigned with Christ a thousand years" (Rev. 20:4-5)—led to a growing association of the role of the millennium—a thousand-year reign—with the other doctrines of eschatology. Within the church there are several types of millennialism, each with its own distinct understanding of the end time and the nature of the church.

Postmillennialism.—Postmillennialism has appeared in various forms since the union of Christianity and the Roman Empire and the anticipation of a golden age of the church which would usher in the kingdom. In this view, the kingdom is already present in the hearts and lives of persons, working through them like leaven to affect the whole world. As the church fulfills its evangelical task under the leadership of the Holy Spirit, the whole of human society is changed. This leads to a great revival of religion and the Christianization of the social order. Such a period of spiritual renewal will precede the second coming of Christ. While this golden age may or may not be a literal thousand years, Christ will not return until *after* the millennium is complete. Hence the proponents of this view are called postmillennialists. The church, therefore, is called to participate with God in bringing in the kingdom. The church is not the kingdom but marks the way to it. It is the means for bringing the gospel of the kingdom to all the world.

Postmillennialism has been an important doctrine of eschatology among Protestant groups both liberal and Evangelical. Jonathan

Edwards, the great Puritan preacher and theologian, believed that the revivals he witnessed in Colonial New England were evidence of the millennial fulfillment. The conversion of multitudes pointed to the golden age of the church and the coming of the kingdom. Edwards even speculated that such a final work would begin in America. In many respects, Jonathan Edwards was the first great American postmillennialist.

Charles G. Finney, the nineteenth-century revivalist, looked upon the awakening of his day as a sign of the kingdom. Finney and his followers promoted a doctrine of Christian perfection which had significant implications for the individual and the society. Personal conversion was directly related to the transformation of all human institutions. The perfectionists who followed Finney worked to abolish slavery, to promote missions, education, and equal rights for women, all with a view to the bringing in the postmillennial kingdom.

More theologically liberal individuals looked to the progressive improvement of the social order as a sign of the immediacy of the kingdom. They preached the need for a social gospel which would convert sinners and society into the image of Christ. Society was progressing toward the kingdom. Scientific and technological improvement were evidence of the progress of the race. From a historical perspective, the death and destruction created by World War I brought a powerful disillusionment to postmillennialism in the twentieth century.

The church plays an important role in postmillennial eschatology. Through its faithful proclamation of the gospel, the church participates with God in the bringing in the kingdom.[16]

Amillennialism.—The amillennial view of eschatology suggests that the millennium is a symbolic or allegorical idea, not a literal thousand-year reign. It represents a spiritualizing of millennial concepts. For amillennialists, the details of Christ's return are less significant than the hope of His coming. The second coming could occur at any moment and does not depend on worldwide evangelization or inevitable progress. Since the millennium is symbolic and spiritual, the end time may occur during a period of either peace or tribulation. Christ's return is not bound to a doctrine of inevitable social progress or decline. The church, therefore, is to live by faith, not by millennial speculation. The church has already received its true spiritual resurrection and judgment. The return of Christ will simply confirm what has already taken place spiritually.[17]

The church is thus called to confirm in its life and witness what it already is, the resurrected community, living already in the new age. Amillennialism seeks to take seriously the millennial language of Revelation 20 as a powerful symbol which helps define the church's identity in the present not merely in some future time.

Premillennialism.—Premillennialism, popular today among many conservative-Evangelical Christians, has a long and complex history in the church. A type of premillennial eschatology was prominent in the early church's expectation of the immediate and cataclysmic return of Christ. Justin Martyr (100?-165?) represents one of the earliest premillennialist postitions in the church. He suggested that Christ would return to establish His earthly kingdom, the new Jerusalem, on the ruins of the old Jerusalem. Christ Himself would bring in the golden age of the kingdom, ending after a thousand years in the final consummation.[18] Literal interpretations of the biblical materials led to excesses which influenced the decline of premillennialism in the church.

By the nineteenth century, premillennialism had experienced a revival among many Christians disillusioned with postmillennial views on progress and amillennial emphasis on the symbolic nature of biblical eschatology. In its basic form, premillennialism suggests that the return of Christ is a literal event which occurs at the beginning of the millennial age. The kingdom is brought in, not by the work of the church or the progress of the human race, but by the supernatural return of the triumphant Christ. For premillennialists, Christ returns in bodily form to establish the kingdom on earth.[19] The signs of the times prior to Christ's coming reflect the increasing moral and spiritual decline of human civilization, not its progress. Premillennialists are essentially literalists in their interpretation of biblical prophecies but disagree as to the time when prophecies are fulfilled.

"Historicist" premillennialists believe that prophetic biblical passages reflect "the entire history of the church in symbolic form." Thus the church's past and present provides clues to "God's prophetic timetable."[20]

"Futurist" premillennialists, on the other hand, suggest that the biblical prophecies have yet to be fulfilled in the latter days. Such prophecies have little relationship to the church, which is merely an interim community which exists between the grand events of Christ's resurrection and triumphant return. As society grows increasingly depraved, the Antichrist gains power, creating a period of great tribulation. At the end of the tribulation, Christ returns, defeating Antichrist and establishing His millennial kingdom at the end of which Satan will be defeated, the judgment will occur, and a new heaven and earth created.[21]

Futurists agree that the church will be "raptured," caught up to be with Christ (1 Thess. 4:15-17), during this prophetic process. They disagree as to the moment when the rapture will occur. Pretribulationists say it will occur prior to the tribulation; midtribulationists say it will occur during the tribulation, while posttribulationists suggest it occurs at the end of that terrible period.

This complex speculation regarding eschatology has led some premillennialists to place the doctrine of the church within a doctrine of dispensationalism—the division of recorded time into special prophetic periods, or dispensations. In this view the church is a provisional people of God, called into existence between Israel's rejection of Christ and the final judgment. Dillard Erickson wrote: "After Israel rejected the kingdom, God offered it to the church. The church was, as it were, God's substitute for Israel, 'grafted in.' The Kingdom for Israel, however, was merely postponed. It will again be offered to God's people, Israel, after the time of the Gentiles is complete. God has not forgotten His people Israel nor displaced them with the church."[22]

In this brief survey, we can see that the various theories of eschatology, particularly premillennialism, have produced diverse doctrines of the church in the context of millennial speculation. Millennial theories come and go in the history of the church. The church's historical circumstances influence the way it understands eschatology. Yet these theories point to the central eschatological issue—hope.

The Community of Hope

"Beloved, we are God's children now; it does not yet appear what we shall be, but we know that when he appears we shall be like him, for we shall see him as he is" (1 John 3:2). Therein is the ground of Christian hope. It is found, not in elaborate speculation as to "what we shall be," but in the confidence that "we shall be like him." The church, therefore, is the community of hope. Its life is not bound to the past or even to the present. The church understands itself and its mission in light of the future. Such hope is not a merely passive characteristic of the church. It is the church's active participation in the future with God. Christian hope, therefore, is not simply to wish for the kingdom; it is the confidence that the kingdom is on its way, indeed, it has already begun through the presence of the Spirit. The Spirit Himself is the pledge, the promise of the future experienced in the present. He is the earnest money of an inheritance not fully received.

As Emil Brunner declared, hope is "the presence of the future," a way in which what will happen begins to happen.[23] "It is hope based upon faith in the activity of God, not . . . upon the self-confidence and self-security of man."[24] Through hope, the church understands its present identity through its participation in the future. It understands what it is, in light of what it will be. So the church's present identity is shaped by its "recollection" of its past and its "expectation" of the future.[25]

Such hope is a mystery, experienced by faith. The faith of the church is not in itself or the inevitable progress of the race, but in the future of God. Hope is the confidence (faith) that God who began "a good work in you will bring it to completion at the day of Jesus Christ" (Phil. 1:6). It is to believe that God who called history into being will have the final word and that the word will be good. So faith and hope are inseparable. "Faith is the foundation of hope," Brunner wrote, and "hope is that which gives content to faith."[26] Through Christian hope, the church faces the future unafraid. It does not lose itself in idle speculation as to the details of the end time, nor is it weakened by the complex problems of this "present evil age." Rather, with confidence in God it is then free to confront whatever life may bring, free to fulfill its mandate to proclaim the gospel to feed the hungry, clothe the naked, and declare the year of the Lord's favor. Paul's words are a declaration of hope for the church in every age:

> We recommend ourselves by the innocence of our behaviour, our grasp of truth, our patience and kindliness; by gifts of the Holy Spirit, by sincere love, by declaring the truth, by the power of God. We wield the weapons of righteousness in right hand and left. Honour and dishonour, praise and blame, are alike our lot: we are the imposters who speak the truth, the unknown men whom all men know; dying we still live on; disciplined by suffering, we are not done to death; in our sorrows who always have cause for joy; poor ourselves, we bring wealth to many; penniless, we own the world (2 Cor. 6:6-10, NEB).

Notes

1. R. W. Kicklighter, "The Origins of the Church," *What Is the Church?* Duke McCall, ed. (Nashville: Broadman Press, 1958), p. 43.

2. Hans Küng, *The Church* (New York: Sheed and Ward, 1967), pp. 47-52.

3. E. Glenn Hinson, *The Integrity of the Church* (Nashville: Broadman Press, 1978), p. 59.

4. Ibid., pp. 60-61; and J. Robert Nelson, *The Realm of Redemption* (Greenwich, Conn.: Seabury Press, 1951), p. 214.

5. C. H. Dodd, *The Apostolic Preaching and Its Developments* (London: Hodder and Stoughten Ltd., 1944), p. 13.

6. Nelson, p. 220.

7. R. Newton Flew, *Jesus and His Church* (New York: Abingdon, 1938), p. 24.

8. Ibid., p. 25.

9. Ibid., p. 33.

10. E. F. Scott, *The Nature of the Early Church,* p. 47.

11. Ibid., p. 37.

12. Nelson, p. 232, citing Karl Barth, *The Resurrection of the Dead* (London: n.p., 1933), pp. 176-180.

13. Claude Welch, *The Reality of the Church* (New York: Charles Scribner's Sons, 1958), p. 209.

14. Küng, p. 59.

15. Gayraud Wilmore, *Last Things First* (Philadelphia: The Westminster Press, 1982), p. 29.

16. Dillard J. Erickson, *Contemporary Options in Eschatology* (Grand Rapids: Baker Book House, 1977), pp. 55-72.

17. Wilmore, pp. 46-47.

18. Erickson, pp. 94-95.

19. Ibid., pp. 91-92.

20. Timothy Weber, *Living in the Shadow of the Second Coming* (New York: Oxford University Press, 1979), pp. 9-10.

21. Ibid., pp. 10-11.

22. Erickson, p. 121.

23. Emil Brunner, *Eternal Hope* (Philadelphia: The Westminster Press, 1954), p. 7.

24. Ibid., p. 17.

25. Welch, p. 143.

26. Brunner, p. 28.

Scripture Index